OF BEING AND OF MEANING

Hans C. Syz

OF BEING AND OF MEANING

Translated from the German by Björn Merker

Philosophical Library
New York

Published 1981 by Philosophical Library, Inc.
200 West 57th Street, New York, N. Y. 10019.
Copyright © 1981 by Hans C. Syz.
All Rights Reserved.
First published under the title
Vom Sein und vom Sinn
copyright © 1972 by Hans C. Syz.
All Rights Reserved.

ISBN 8022-2374-5
Library of Congress Catalogue Card Number 80-82648

Preface

WHEN I WROTE these notes in May, 1916, I was a twenty-one year old medical student engaged in preclinical work in Zürich, Switzerland, where I was born and where I spent my early years. My parents were of old Swiss stock and I was raised in a conventional Protestant setting. Questioning many accepted tenets of my background I passed through long periods of search and conflict preceding the experience reported here.

As will be evident, the notes were not written for publication; they emerged from the need for clarification when I was faced with a powerful experience for which no avenues of communication seemed available other than writing. Thus came about a spontaneous account of a potent event which was stirring and meaningful to me and which had relevance to a whole array of perennial problems of life and existence. In expressing my thoughts I did not adhere to an established philosophy or to the teachings of a preceptor.

I had not re-read these notes for decades, but a few months ago when I went over some of the pages I found their content still meaningful. A number of people whose judgment I value have now seen this material and they have suggested that it be made generally available. The notes are given here without alteration or commentary.

Hans C. Syz
Westport, Connecticut

OF BEING AND OF MEANING

May 14, 1916
Sunday

I SHOULD LIKE to put down a few things concerning my present condition. Thursday night, May 4th, I repeatedly awoke with a feeling of great terror combined with a certain train of thought. Naturally I do not know whether the emergence of these thoughts was primary,

1

causing the fear, or whether the fear had bodily origins, bringing about the thoughts. It should also be noted that I did some rowing on Wednesday but not on Thursday, on which day I only took a sunbath in very hot weather. I had already experienced the welling up of similar anxiety and a similar complex of thoughts once earlier this summer in the Tenigerbad, but was able to repress it as soon as it arose.

The content of the arising series of thoughts can be described as the sudden insight into the total relativity of all existence, especially of all forms emanating from man. As this applies also to our forms of thought, thinking as it were dissolves itself—which may in part explain my feeling of terror. This, of course, describes only one side of my inner experience. One could also say that suddenly I sensed deeply the question of the meaning of life in its entirety. Or, the question arose: what is the essential nature of man, of consciousness, of personality? For I have always been occupied with these problems; I simply could not live life as it came. I had to give account to myself for what I did; I sought to discover my real self in order to guide my actions according to my true nature. Thus, many of the things of practical life did not interest me very much. I was not sociable; that is, I could not really or fully enjoy the simple things of life as long as the one big question remained unanswered.

Faced with this one great question, everyday life

seemed of very little value, and I was unable to understand how a man could be content to be, for example, simply a coachman; I was amazed at the lack of meaning of such a way of life. And now, the full realization suddenly descends upon me that the question cannot be answered at all, that the various solutions are merely external formulations without any corresponding content in reality.

This outcome may be due to my very critical nature which tested any opinion and its opposite with equal ruthlessness. Were I able to embrace one form unconditionally, I should be saved. But though at present I do not lack sensitiveness, I do not have any strong unilateral feeling.

My greatest current anxiety stems, I think, from suddenly having discovered that the foundation of personality is a nothing, that the human soul is simply compounded of feelings and thoughts, and what I sought beyond this does not exist at all. Thus everything suddenly appears alien, life ultimately incomprehensible. I know that, while my thoughts and conclusions may be logically correct, my mind nonetheless enters a track which is not normal in everyday life. It no longer corresponds to the forms which life happens to follow and demand.

It seems as though there were another type of consciousness besides the ordinary one. Often it appears to me that I have lived in a dream thus far and that other people live in a sleep-consciousness which cannot be abandoned, however, without despairing. Perhaps I am currently striving to escape from dangerous thoughts by escaping into unconsciousness. The strange condition has come upon me especially in sleep and several times I have awakened with great anxiety. During the day I was often quite as usual but never losing a certain anguish, a certain pressure in my head. The whole condition has gradually increased since its inception, although I really fought against it with all my powers. Since last night it has manifested itself primarily as a strong feeling of tension, an inner disquiet to the point of bursting. It would not let me sleep calmly and robbed me of my appetite.

Perhaps I shall be able to overcome this crisis by expressing what moves me. Also, it may have gone this far because I never could talk over my numerous inner struggles with anyone. Unfortunately, I never could bring up such things with my parents as they simply would not have comprehended them. Or, without the possibility of understanding, they simply would have confronted my thoughts with their own educationally slanted views. Large areas of thought which have occupied me a great deal do not exist for my parents, and in that respect my being understood by them is precluded. This has caused me great pain.

TODAY, MAY 15TH, my experience no longer put me in such an unhappy condition as had been the case part of yesterday, Sunday. I regained the confidence and hope that after all this crisis would be brought to a favorable conclusion. The extraordinary tension of the day before had subsided, and I felt only something like a pressure, as though the train of thoughts regarding the experience, without becoming conscious, obstructed the free flow of other thoughts. It was as though my being could not give itself undivided and wholly to the thoughts that arose, but was in some of its feeling governed by another central complex.

I now fully understood what Schiller felt in his poem "The Veiled Statue at Sais" ("Das verschleierte Bild zu Sais"), where he presents the confrontation with truth as something so dreadful. I felt that I had penetrated as deeply as man can, that the end-point of all my striving had been reached not by discovering some final fundamental thought but by having arrived at the nature of thought itself beyond which all thinking ceases. This recognition was not intellectual recognition but altogether an experience—complete reality. It is, therefore, extraordinarily difficult for me to express these ultimates in the usual forms of interchange whose purely formal significance was just what I experienced. I know with certainty that no philosophy can take me deeper than this, as my experience took place in a sphere which cannot be contained within a section of any science, but rather encompasses within itself all philosophy, or better, the possibility of all philosophy.

My experience concerns not only the nature of reason

sought to recognize completely—I now suddenly realized that there is no such "I" at all; this too is only a concept, a form, which comes to be taken for granted by us through habituation. I recognized that the soul or the "I" consists of the states, feelings, and thoughts that variously move us, and that its content is nothing permanent or lasting.

All of reality lies within me only. Something outside of me will, of course, correspond to it but this something in its very nature is totally incomprehensible to me. All that I regard as world, as external reality, is nothing but inner states within me. By linking these inner states with language and other shared forms of expression they are to a certain extent objectified. Existence which actually lies only within ourselves is carried to the outside. It is language which makes thought possible at all. The merging of internal states with external forms is what constitutes thought. And because a very specific character and combination of thoughts is common to a large number of people, these thoughts are taken to be quite natural, without any further question regarding their actual content.

In our times the importance of relativity has of course been discovered at many points, and this takes place somewhat as follows: cognitively one reaches the conclusion that certain forms of thought or opinions (for exam-

and its functions, but encompasses life in general—all of existence. In a sense it contains all of reality, and in whatever way I may express myself, it sets the limits for man's possible knowledge regarding thought, consciousness, life, personality, soul, and the meaning of life.

I recognized clearly that all thinking finally is feeling. This again can be said only in forms of thought and hence it is very questionable whether one will be understood.

ON MONDAY, MAY 15th, I was particularly m
the complete change in the view of man which
had taken hold of me. While before I had se
stance in man—an "I" which I had tried to
ever greater awareness within myself and wh

9

ple, some form of religion) are incorrect. However, this does involve the error, 1) of viewing, for instance, a form of religion as merely an opinion of the person concerned, whereas for him it represents the real, the actually existing situation (or a part of it), 2) of offering one's own view as possessing a *higher degree of reality* compared to the false, "fantastic" view of the other person, without realizing that one's own views and feelings are of the same ideality as those of the other. One simply does not realize that all that we call world, all our thoughts including the concept of *existence* (and its accompanying internal state) are throughout of ideal (that is, figmental) nature. Thus I came to experience that existence generally will remain wholly and always a puzzle.

What strikes me as inexplicable is not any particular question, such as the meaning of life, or how one could conceive all the qualities of the grown individual to be contained in the egg-cell, but the incomprehensibility of the most elementary event, for example, the movement of waves on a lake (or the relationship of any event to my consciousness). The development of the ovum does not appear strange to an accomplished scientist. He will describe the whole process and in so doing will believe he has explained it. Another, not so familiar with scientific thought, may nonetheless notice that the scientist simply substitutes specific names for certain manifestations of

11

the developmental process, and then connects and logically aligns these forms of thought with already existing forms of thinking. The phenomena thus come within the reach of rational thought but are not comprehended in any way as to their essential nature.

A more deeply penetrating way of looking at things permits us to realize that man is related to the simplest and most natural events just as he is to those which still appear incomprehensible to us. Man has, however, become so accustomed to identifying certain internal states with self-created forms of thought, to objectifying them, and is so actively supported by linguistic convention, that the recognition of the pervasive ideality of all existence becomes very difficult. The final and unconditional truth, the ultimate base, becomes clear to him only through inner experience.

On Monday, May 15th, I had to observe above all the human "I" from this viewpoint. I recognized, or rather felt, how the "I" actually exists only in the fixed forms of thought set by ourselves, but that in fact it is founded on something quite different, that its basis is nothing but motion. I felt that the "I" really consists only of thoughts, feelings, and inner states—beyond these there is no further unmoving core, no encompassing substance. This inner experience may be expressed only with the greatest difficulty. It did not consist in any new view of the nature of the soul but in sensing the nature of that through which we arrive at conceptions, for instance, of the soul, at consciousness, at thinking, at any stable formulation—at a process which in itself really cannot be expressed through any of these formulations.

Truly, it is not possible to penetrate to the inward being of another person. We really do not grasp exactly what feelings live in a fellow man. Even if he expresses them verbally, this stimulates only *one's own* inner states which are tied to the words of conventional language. Usually we simply identify these inner states with those of the other, without recognizing that in reality the latter are something external to us and by their very nature unreachable. They may even qualitatively represent something very different from our inner feelings in spite of common external expression.

I felt very clearly the utter determinism of man's life, that his entire inner life in a sense runs its course in a reflex manner. This was particularly clear to me Monday night in the chemical-physiological laboratory where I noticed and understood every move of my fellow laboratory students in this light. Everyone is willing to assume an unconditional causality in animals. But even here, behind its higher functions, the "person" of the animal manifests itself as the substance from which certain acts are assumed to flow purposefully. This view imposes itself especially in those instances where the ways of the animal appear to be intelligent or purposeful, where it is a matter of ordering or inhibiting "natural" instincts.

In man, feeling and acting are accompanied by consciousness, and this maintains in us a belief in our own freedom. But the clearest consciousness, which also allows the strongest feeling of freedom to arise, is only imagined. It consists in the circumstance that inner conditions brought about by external and internal events are linked with each other in a generally valid way and accompanied by the images of language, thus giving rise to thoughts which we take to be outer reality. Through these thoughts we believe we comprehend events, although they only represent self-created symbols and forms accompanying an otherwise incomprehensible process. We believe we recognize existing things and processes by consciousness and thought, whereas we really have no possibility of grasping the nature of things. Many of the concepts arising from artificial delimitation will perhaps always be retained for practical reasons (for example, the "I" of conventional language). But one will have to realize the ideality of many of the forms of thought derived in this way, in order not to get entangled in too marked contradictions.

The concept of "freedom of will," for example, is wholly built on the idea of "I," wholly of symbolic nature, and when naively taken as reality, it is completely untenable. The "I" supposedly administers its will by free choice, as though it could use it somehow as a tool. Here it immediately becomes evident that the separation between "I" and "will," their delimitation and characterization, their juxtaposition, the treatment of will as though it were a separate personality—this does not occur in the actual flow of events. It is merely a formulation which man has imposed on events.

Through simple rational thought on this theme one may reach the following conclusion: if free will stands for complete arbitrariness, one is not speaking of freedom but of lawlessness. To assume this is impossible, for we would have to desist from all thinking, from any statement about whatever lies within the scope of thoughts. Hence, will cannot be regarded as an isolated lawless entity, but is generally assumed to be dependent on the "I." It is in a sense regarded as the outflow of the personality, and as such it cannot any longer claim freedom. That is, the problem shifts, and the question arises: is the "I" free? With this the artificial division of "I" and "will" becomes clearly apparent—"will" after all being an important component of the "I."

We speak of freedom only in relation to action, or to the will upon which action is based. Will, however, exists not as an isolated entity, but must be aligned within and is dependent upon other patterns. These complex patterns in turn—established either through their own lawfulness or external influence—are what make up our "I" and it is not possible to assume a further, independent, let alone dominating "I" beyond them. Free will can only be interpreted as a very specific direction of will that really accords with our own nature and is not determined by a variety of external chance events. It is the outflow of the "I" which, of course, is wholly determined by inner and outer factors.

It must be clear how thoughts come to us, one linking to the other, or evoked by external situations. Caprice, that is, lawlessness, the absence of causality, cannot be assumed here; it would not deserve the name of freedom anyway. We are often not capable of perceiving the basis from which our feelings and thoughts arise but recognize more easily that our behavior is simply the expression, the result of internal excitation and external circumstances. In view of the tremendous richness of the forms thus arising and their infinite possibilities of combination, it usually is difficult to comprehend that all this necessarily has a cause and is absolutely determined. I did not arrive at this conclusion rationally, but I *felt* it, I experienced it directly by virtue of a somewhat different attitude towards life that gave me a deep insight into the nature of consciousness to which we owe all concepts with which we operate rationally. This consciousness is what we cannot get outside of. There is no "I" standing above it, guiding and influencing its laws at its own discretion. But we may seek to know the limits of this consciousness, and if we have a sense of its nature, we may seek expression thereof in the forms created by it.

We do not walk, we are being carried; this was what I experienced quite directly.

MONDAY NIGHT, MAY 22nd, we attended a very beautiful organ recital in the cathedral where Durigo sang, and under the feelings and thoughts that arose the tension and pressure which for some time had been with me dissolved. I now experienced with total clarity as

19

ultimate and actual reality that which over a period of perhaps ten years had from time to time taken possession of me as the highest of feelings. I might express it as an inmost feeling of infinity or of the general relativity through which the appearances and things of life that usually are taken for granted suddenly appear quite foreign and in essence incomprehensible. My experience was in a sense what under different circumstances is designated as ecstasy; there, too, man has a different attitude toward existence. He gets an intimation of the merely relative nature of what usually passes as reality, but then interprets this intimation specifically in relation to established religious forms.

The intimation in question actually stands above all religion in so far as religion purports to be more than inexpressible feeling, namely a demarcation, a specific conceptual formulation. The experience I had, after all, embodies the nature and limits of concept and thought, and thus of what is real for us (also in the sphere of religion). It cannot be expressed and transmitted to others directly but only through these forms. This naturally poses exceptional difficulties, as verbally expressed thoughts have primarily a cognitive-rational effect and only rarely manage to convey the feeling, the inner and wholly real life from which they spring. It is quite impossible for "normal" man who is completely adjusted to prevailing forms—and who usually is the thoroughly average man—to see the world also from the other side. All too long has he uncritically absorbed reality as his surroundings see it. His being is already too habituated to and absorbed in a particular form of existence to even conceive of, let alone experience, its symbolic nature. He, therefore, will not be able to understand a view that differs from his own, or he may even relegate it to the realm of pathology, which is the most convenient, but also a very narrow course of action.

The separation of body and mind may be necessary and practical for common language and thought. However, the view that sees them as realities, different in a deeper sense, cannot be maintained. Our body, its various parts and organs, is just as much part of our "I" as the mental functions. The two realms are in most intimate mutual relationship. We assign them to a particular domain of being according to the relations and forms in which they appear to us. It is our organizing thought which somehow assigns two basic substances—one material, one mental—to an extremely intricate process. This demarcation possesses reality only for those who live within these forms of thought. But it is not possible to regard the body as something natural and the mind as something supernatural. We perceive something as natural only because it is commonly couched in definite forms of thought, because we have recognized a definite lawfulness in its manner of appearance, because it stands in a constant and familiar relationship to us.

Thus gravity, for example, is taken as something completely natural. We recognize that it always operates according to the same rules and is active in and around us at every moment. Yet, who can really tell what gravity is? Who really grasps what this attraction of masses, operative at infinite distances, actually means? Matter influenced across empty space without a mediating link? Does not this make it evident that the term "force" is merely a concept, a label or form that we have attached to something completely unknown to us, to a "something" just as amazing, just as supernatural as any mental phenomenon, for example a thought? The difference lies primarily in the nature and number of relationships that are known to us concerning these different phenomena. Our understanding of their actual nature is entirely missing in both. Any ordering of these phenomena in the forms of our language means an estrangement from absolute reality, compensated, however, by letting the phenomena enter into the only reality possible for us, and of whose nature (that is, its ideality) we should become aware.

The example of gravity, whose nature is beyond our understanding (in spite of its ever-present and lawful workings and possible explanatory and descriptive theories), will be understood by many people, but many will find it impossible to extend this perspective to the very ordinary appearances and events that confront us in daily life. They believe that existence is arranged and delimited according to familiar terms such as mind, matter, energy, mechanism, etc., not only in their thought, but also in a reality beyond or above thinking. As we tragically cannot transcend ourselves and are able to express ourselves regarding these ultimates only in the forms given by our language, we can view them only symbolically.

Events in and around us are in their essential nature completely incomprehensible, something the true content of which we never will get at. The life within has effects outside of us, and the forces of the world impinge upon us. There is no reason to believe that the workings of the cosmos are of a different nature from the workings within ourselves—everywhere related force and form. The religious expression of this view would be pantheism: in everything we find divine action, God in all that occurs. But this, too, is only a form through which we attempt to grasp what is past comprehension. Theism, too, is such a form, and as such (when it does not fossilize) is as valuable as any other formula, especially as from our standpoint it also may be justified by another

23

consideration: having penetrated somewhat into the nature of personality and consciousness, and having recognized in them a specifically ordered interplay of energy and form, which process ultimately remains incomprehensible, one could assume a similarity in the totality of events, namely a personal, conscious quality.

From the basis of my experience many contradictions are resolved that we otherwise cannot understand. From this background I grasped the *nature and greatness of Christ* with particular clarity. I am convinced that the inner experience which was the mainspring of his personality and life must have been very similar to my experience, notwithstanding that—according to different circumstances—it expressed itself in different forms. The deepest meaning remains the same.

The center in Christ's life was God, who for him was not a concept or doctrine which can be believed, but a reality, a living presence. The person of Jesus embodied an intense feeling of what lies beyond the forms that for us represent reality. Consciousness (or subconsciousness) of the nonrational was always present within him. This gave his inner life direction, not as a system of thought, but as experience, as *his* reality. Only secondarily did he give it commonly understandable forms in accordance with the spirit of his time and his own capacity of expression. The basic motive to which we can return I would call—in accordance with *my* way of discriminating—the experience of the *ideality of reality*. From this basis, to put it differently, Christ drew the power for his personality and work. This underlying experience was somehow always present within him, effective as a guiding agent.

If one strips the incidental from the endeavors, from the deeper creations and statements of religious men, of artists and other creative people, one can easily understand that here are attempts to grasp and in some way express a basic truth which may be implicitly interwoven as a latent thought. From this point of view it becomes possible to fully understand the certainty and spontaneity with which Jesus followed his unusual path. Many people never grasp this and believe him to be very different from us humans, a "godlike" being; or they scornfully shrug him off as a visionary. True, Christ was an idealist, but so are all of us, and his "ideals" were as real to him as what we believe to be reality. As Christ did not compulsively pursue ideals (which only we from another viewpoint call "ideals") but lived in them as his reality, the great simplicity and spontaneity of his speech and action become easily understandable. This is the reason why he generated so strong an influence. Men after all sensed the great truth with which they were confronted, its kinship to their own inner life. Christ found ways to express his primordial experience in forms accessible to other men; he linked his insight to life and drew the practical inferences from it. As an ever present reality his insight gave him the strength for its unimpeded realization. These factors—deepest experience, ability to express it in life, and consistency and wholeness of thought and action—are characteristics of the great person. When some of these characteristics are missing, nothing remains but to join an accepted and available way of life. One has to adjust to given compromises, if one neither feels the necessity nor has the ability in any area to overcome them.

Thus it is easy to understand that Christ regarded with a certain indifference the forms of his surroundings, that is, the prejudices, opinions, customs, institutions, in short all that his contemporaries had taken over from their ancestors and had woven into their life as reality. His standpoint was simply at a higher level. His work was in certain respects a transcendence of these forms. Expressed in today's language, he had a feeling of the merely relative meaning of all forms. Although justifiable and even absolutely necessary, these forms nonetheless imply a limitation; they can become one of man's strongest bondages, if shortsightedly regarded as absolute reality in one of their specialized, one-sided manifestations. Actually they may have strayed far from essentials and have lost the connection with the deeper life. In this sense, Christ was far more revolutionary than is commonly thought, as seen for example in his attitude towards the recognized authority of the scribes, towards the ritual forms (prayer, fasting, alms, Sabbath, etc.), his relationship to tradition and the mighty authority of the laws (". . . but I say unto you . . ."), his freedom regarding prevailing custom (the publican, the adulteress). But with all this he did not exceed certain limits. He found for himself suitable forms which he was able to tie in with those already in existence. He did not formulate his standpoint in such isolation as to lose touch with life.

This indifference to and nondependence upon forms are closely connected with a deep appreciation of just this formative quality in man. From the feeling of the true (namely limited) significance of form springs comprehension of its various manifestations. Hence the wide vision with which Christ approached men, whom he did not divide and judge according to any scheme or formula. The rigid separation of men into good and bad, converts and unbelievers, plays a major role in religions, including Christianity, although it is not in accordance with Christ's spirit at all. His greatness consists in seeing beyond incidental forms (that is, evaluating them according to their true significance), which does not have to mean acceptance of every form.

From this elevated viewpoint he was able to regard every other human being as equal to himself, to love him, even in his distorted expressions. Christ's love is the altogether simple, practical result of his deepest experience. The social interaction among people, this most important expression of life, is inhibited, narrowed, made superficial, through all kinds of forms, and is led in a direction not at all reaching, but rather contradicting, the deepest nature of man. Christ showed as a natural expression of his personality a way of interaction through which the restricting influence of form may be overcome. Where his love is active, people can again make immediate contact with each other. His love is, however, more than what is known as humanitarianism, more than pity and compassion with which good Christians often believe they may rest content. It is rather a frame of mind, a mode of viewing the world and man, an approach which consistently takes "judge not" as a premise, and builds on that. This form of love is altogether natural when it is a feeling-attitude, the result of inner experience.

One tries to recapture this inner experience through enacting the religious forms used by Christ. Of course this is not fully possible for anyone, and thus one is often left with mere external religious dogmas to which love, also as a dogma, is only superficially related, lacking its actual source of strength. Hence it does not become the deep feeling-conviction or all-pervasive method, but at a critical moment turns into a fiasco. It consists of a behavior learned for all kinds of situations following up various love commandments of Jesus. We are lucky nonetheless that there are ways through which we may attain the frame of mind that leads to the love of Christ. But these ways do not have to consist in copying the forms in which Christ expressed his religious experience which today are far from guaranteeing the presence of this experience itself.

In a unified concept and unfolding of life it is necessary to consider and organically encompass all the realities that face and closely concern us, including the phenomenon we label "death." Death, that is, the fear of death, is one of the strongest forces in our life, and every man seeks somehow to overcome this fear. Some do this by the assertion, by the belief that death actually does not exist, that what is meant by dying—cessation of life, of consciousness, of personality—all this does not take place when death occurs. It only *appears* so, but in reality the individual continues to exist. This opinion maintains itself on the basis of the customary cleavage of body and mind, but gets entangled in vivid contradictions within its own contentions as soon as it claims to be more than intuition or feeling, namely, a detailed, logical, intellectual definition.

Another way of overcoming the fear of death appears in the effort simply to forget about it, to ignore it. One talks as little as possible about death, seeks to remove it from our life as a determining factor, tries to keep away all thoughts from this theme. If nonetheless forced to consider it, this will be done in forms that are generally current and thus the phenomenon of death appears as something wholly self-evident, not at all strange. Incessant mental pursuits, work, entertainment, and other diverting activities may be means of keeping away from the dreaded deeper contemplation of the secret of death.

The fear of death must indeed be overcome if we want to let our capacities come to full development and enactment. To overcome it by any kind of forgetting, however, is only superficial, fictitious. It does not hold up against stronger storms, nor does it suffice for someone who is searching more deeply. The other way of overcoming the fear of death—its reinterpretation or even denial—fulfilled its purpose and was an organic part of the world of thought and feeling from which it sprang, a world which however is no longer with us. Our sense of reality and truth demands that we conceive of things exactly as they present themselves—consideration of practical living cannot force us to compromise.

I, for one, could never share the common opinion that sees nothing incomprehensible in death, that seems fully to understand this phenomenon. When other people spoke of death as though its nature and import were perfectly clear to them, I had to say to myself that I did not understand this phenomenon. In spite of being used to the sight of dead people, death itself remained an incomprehensible puzzle to me. Now I know that I then felt that all thoughts men may have on death and in which they live as self-evident reality, are only inadequate expressions, a giving form to something of which the essential content is unreachable.

Death is only one particular and especially important event which can draw our attention with great force and clarity to the incomprehensible, the puzzling, that is equally manifest in all other events of the world. Certainly we must incorporate the idea of death into our system of thought, into our consciousness, but this must occur from within. Especially he who searches more deeply, who wants to shape his life to a unity, who must maintain a certain consistency, cannot rest content with fitting the very important phenomenon of death haphazardly into his thinking. He must harmoniously integrate

31

integrated into the totality, utterly lost its terror and was no longer aversive to me.

Such experience, such immediate life, is not always present. But the insights arising in those moments can maintain their effect in a life that proceeds in accordance with customary norms and familiar trends of thought, if one succeeds in incorporating these insights appropriately into prevailing ways of thinking. If we thus reach a reconciliation with death not by repressing the thoughts concerning it, but by properly fitting them into our consciousness, we do not any longer have to seek explanations for the unknowable to which only the misguided fear of death can drive us. Rather, we may again turn fully and with sober joy to life.

The spiritually active will at times ask the question: does life actually have meaning? Many will simply turn the question down as superfluous and beyond the realm of common thought, declare it to be meaningless, and rid themselves of it in adjustment to the surrounding world which is not confused by such thoughts. Referring to sound common sense, they will answer this question in the positive. They are even able to give a detailed exposition of the meaning of life, for example with regard to a certain development which would show the striving towards a dominant final goal. Or from a religious standpoint they see the demands and promises of their creed as the final objective to be reached, even presuming to find it only in another coming life.

Not everyone is satisfied with disposing of the question in this manner, and one tries to arrive at a real answer by other means, namely by testing the known facts without preconceptions and therefrom drawing one's conclusions. What goal does mankind strive for? Is there really a final purpose that could give meaning to our life? Is there a final value upon which our value systems can be built? Here one must submit that we cannot know what is decided, what still may come to pass, what man is still to attain. Nonetheless, the factual examination of the above questions must ultimately arrive at a pessimistic conclusion. It is very questionable whether man as a whole will develop towards a specific goal. It seems more probable that single nations or whole cultures will reach a certain peak of development, live through a golden age, perhaps even achieve a desired total integration, but that this again will be followed by periods of disintegration and decay. So that finally we are faced with nothing but changes of forms and their bearers, without any change principally directed toward *one* goal. And even if this—concluded from the history of man up to now— should not happen, if mankind really were to continue growing in a very specific direction, we must still consider that this earth will at some time turn cold. Mankind then must slowly become extinct, and thereby all the values created by it will vanish. Hence there would be no absolute final purpose, nothing permanent that would endow our lives with meaning.

Indeed, meaning really cannot enter into our life from the outside. Human feeling distinguishes different values, and accordingly thought can determine a definite order and suborder of values which direct behavior (or which may result from the observation of behavior). Thus the notion of purpose arises—purposeful development, movement, change. But one cannot extend arbitrarily this kind of observation to all of mankind or even to the world at large, as this way of looking at things is only a practical mental device with which we can accompany our own feeling and acting. Seen in isolation without reference to man, it does not readily have validity for phenomena of different nature, for example "change" or "process" in general, so that "world events" may not be viewed at all in such a perspective. Thus it is erroneous to assume a future purpose outside of mankind, according to which purpose it would develop. Without taking account of its limits and relativity one cannot simply extend practical thought to the total situation. But if one wants to consider the totality in the perspective of purpose, it is a mistake to conceive of this purpose as a particular, lasting content that eventually will be attained in the course of millennia.

Not outside of us, but within us lies the meaning of life. In life itself lies its meaning. That life is lived at all, that is its meaning. In the instincts, feelings, drives, intents lies the purpose. From them can be derived an order of values accessible to thought which may take the forms of ethics. These can then treat its content in a theoretically consistent manner and posit it as a goal outside of us (yet to be achieved). This is never to be thought of, however, as an absolute, final purpose. If we look beyond the irreducible premises of ethics for motives to which these premises may be traced, we shall not find this ultimate purpose in an even further removed, all-embracing final goal, but only in ourselves, in our internal conditions, in the interplay of our powers. Thus every moment in itself gains meaning. Seen from this viewpoint, there is no longer any principal difference among the lives of individuals: measured in absolute terms all life lacks meaning; from the only possible, relative standpoint there is value and purpose in every human life.

Whether the ethics of an individual are shared by a large or small group of fellow men, whether he contributes much or little to the attainment of a (relative) goal, is not of any fundamental importance here. In case we should not rest content with ethics evolved from our predisposition and circumstances, but seek to deduce it from a conceptual foundation, this foundation must be rooted in a profound (of course one-sided) formulation of life, as we see in life itself the attainment of purpose. From such a formulation, guidelines can then be drawn for the different areas and facets of life. This does not mean that an abstract, logically consistent ethics should be erected on a particular idea, overturning all other value judgments. Ethics after all exist prior to being conceptually formulated.

All formulations, all translations into forms of thought, show a certain independence, a certain constancy. This is true also for ethical forms and demands which continue to exist even if they are no longer in accord with the tendencies from which they once developed. In order that ethics—in practice as well as in theory—do not become lost in incidentals, entangled in estranged forms, their conceptual point of departure has to be taken as deeply as possible. Then they do not remain a worthless abstraction, but represent an attempt to synchronize concept with life as it is, to understand and gather at a nodal point the given forces and operations of life. In this way we are enabled to erect also in our thinking goals and ideals that take account of reality and correspond to our true nature. Thus we may avoid incoherent conceptual side roads (which might be logically deduced, but in this process have lost touch with actuality), and leave behind what has been uncomprehendingly conserved.

Conscious life consists in form taking shape out of the unknown. Form is to be tried in all its possibilities—that is the ultimate purpose. From the basic proposition that the unfathomable in its variations has the possibility of assuming its own form, and that form reaches its highest value only as expression of a corresponding content—from this basis further guidelines may be obtained. This does not immediately set up a specific content, but rather gives a method according to which existing factors should be understood and directed. All existing tendencies are thus taken into account, and *positive* ethics are born that do not waste effort in seeking to repress and stifle irrepressible forces. Rather they place these forces in a new light, and guide them along a healthy course in accord with a superior regulating principle. Thus we may arrive at ethics which really can be lived, as they do not ignore facts because of a false sense of guilt. Being theoretically consistent, their practical application does not have to rest on compromises only.

THIS SPRING I found it particularly painful that contemporary man lacks style, lacks a sweeping guiding orientation. Each of us is wasting much energy in finding his own style, and in so doing we still have not found any bond connecting us to the great majority of people. Even he who easily joins some kind of movement does not get the feeling of really being internally connected with the totality of his own people. Earlier—perhaps eight years ago—I used to ask myself if there were not some specific way of looking at things that was absolutely right, if it really were not possible that all men, being built and functioning in the same way, could share the same basic outlook. I then saw that such a sameness was unattainable, that feeling and thought were not the same in everyone, and that an assumption of a basic truth connecting everyone must meet with great difficulties. In this way no unity was possible, yet I hoped it would be attainable by one means or another. I thought that if it were possible to grasp the world, our thoughts, etc., in a different perspective, to comprehend it from a new point of view, behold it in another way—these otherwise inextricable contradictions would have to unsnarl and join in a new unity. Such a new way of looking at things results from my experience which allowed me to sense deeply the ideality of reality, life appearing as a symbol.

From this viewpoint the variations of thoughts, opinions, and styles of life become comprehensible. They no longer appear as different realities standing isolated and irreconcilable beside each other, but only as different forms of expression in which the otherwise incomprehensible becomes manifest. This varies according to the individual. It enters the most varied relationships and so its symbols change, the internal laws of which further complicate matters. If one has access only to the view which uncritically assigns absolute, self-contained value to the forms current among us, fundamental differences will appear regarding many questions, especially those of ultimate importance. The contradictions will simply not let themselves be disentangled, as though in actual fact different kinds of realities were confronting each other. Proceeding, however, from a different basis of experiencing and viewing the nature of imagination and thought and the reality resulting therefrom, even the deepest contradictions resolve in a higher encompassing unity.

Art, philosophy, science, are attempts at making comprehensible to us the incomprehensible flow of events. This creative activity is not just occasionally evoked in supernormal man through misery and struggle but is a general necessity of life. The world around us and the life within us are simply not as fixed and demarcated as we habitually assume. It is the sameness and relative constancy of our forms of expression, particularly language, which mislead us to believe this. Reality is not exhausted by our normal modes of thought but merely expressed in fragments. Sensitive individuals feel clearly that available forms are insufficient for their inner life. They encounter an altogether different, deeper reality than most

of their fellows and they have to master this as yet unap-
prehended reality. They have to make it comprehensible
and usable in order to maintain the balance of their mental life, their consciousness. If such a capacity for giving
form is present, it will show itself in a work of art or
some other creative act.

However, most people possess so much ability to adjust to prevailing forms that they are not forced to create
new ones. Creativity traces back to the same motivating
principle that finally also is the basis of religion, the intuition or experience of the *formal* character of all that
enters into our consciousness. If we regard this as the
ultimate source of religion, then a shift takes place in the
otherwise fundamental distinction between the religious
and the irreligious person. A principal distinction would
then rather have to be made between people who are
geared entirely to the absolute value of what appears
real to us, and others who somehow (not at all just in
forms of thought) show a deeper understanding. But here
transitions and gradual differences appear on every hand
and distinctions really based on principle are hard to
draw.

There is a tremendous overrating of the capacities of
the intellect in certain circles today, not only subjecting
all existing conditions to warranted criticism but beyond
this bogging down in a veritable intellectual dogmatism.

From youth on the intellectual approach is inculcated into us to such an extent that many of us completely absorb the conviction of its all-sufficiency and somehow never get beyond this limitation. If the intellectual method is consistently carried through, however, one would arrive at a philosophical consideration of those deeper problems which in my view finally should lead to a delineation of the limits of this method. It should lead to a final awareness, to an ultimate experience, which we could perhaps call mystic or religious. For instance, the philosophy of Plato with its praise of the idea culminates in such an experience.

The overrating of the conceptual method is also clearly evident in different religions, for example, in reformed Christianity. Although the deepest source of religion can be seen in the feeling for the limitations of all conceptual definition, the rational method still occupies too large a space in many religions and thus contradictions arise. The issues of religion are elaborated rationally and dogmatism comes about, a form of belief with definite conceptual content. Other expressions of religion disappear, namely those not only based on reason but on art, for instance. The mystical element recedes into the background. The general feeling of the primal event is forced into an exactly delimited religious formula which now represents a sharply separated, self-sustaining area of human life and, therefore, cannot any longer be a penetrating and orienting force.

The excessive emphasis on reason seems to be a characteristic of the male who by nature has at his disposal more free energy than the female. He, therefore, has been able to develop the intellectual aspect of his nature to a greater extent. This perhaps has made possible the higher development of culture, but on the other hand the life of the male has lost in wholeness. In comparison the life of the female—as that of the child—appears more original, unified. She still possesses a surer feeling for the actual value and integration of the realities streaming forth from thought. Not that the female has arrived at the rational insight into the limits of reason which is the given philosophical method of the male. Instinctively she protects herself against any overrating of thought; she inherently does not get lost in such disjointed one-sidedness.

Similarly a more original mode of life may be seen in the early stages of man as exemplified in his myths. In these we have recognized certain "false" personifications and may feel justified in smiling about them. In doing this we do not remember that in our own thought, language, and life, we continually undertake similar personifications, and that those of the old cultures perhaps were more to the point in some respects. The ancestor, worshipping the sun or moon as his god, thereby still displays the original feeling that recognizes everywhere the same inherent workings. Whether out in the world or within man, all existence is recognized as a unity, an intimately interwoven play of forces which cannot be separated and are all equally incomprehensible. And thus we, too, in the deepest sense are an inseparable constituent of the cosmos, equal in our nature to all other events.

The Critical Idiom
General Editor: JOHN D. JUMP

20 Primitivism

Primitivism/ *Michael Bell*

Methuen & Co Ltd

First published 1972
by Methuen & Co Ltd
11 New Fetter Lane, London EC4
© *1972 Michael Bell*
Printed in Great Britain
by Cox & Wyman Ltd, Fakenham, Norfolk

SBN 416 07890 7 Hardback
SBN 416 07900 8 Paperback

Distributed in the U.S.A.
by Barnes & Noble Inc.

For SUSAN

Contents

Acknowledgements

I would like to thank Professor Jump for extending me the hospitality of this series and for his continuing interest in this essay. I also thank my wife for her unfailing help and support in this as in all things.

Permission to quote from copyright sources has been given by the following:

Dover Publications Inc. (*Language and Myth* by Ernst Cassirer); Faber & Faber Ltd (*Complete Poems and Plays of T. S. Eliot* and *The Inheritors* by William Golding); Harcourt Brace Jovanovich Inc. (*Complete Poems and Plays of T. S. Eliot* and *The Inheritors*); Alfred A. Knopf Inc. (*The Plumed Serpent* by D. H. Lawrence); The Macmillan Company (*Collected Poems of W. B. Yeats*); William Morrow & Co. Inc. (*Herman Melville* by Newton Arvin); W. W. Norton & Co. Inc. (*Moby Dick* by Herman Melville); Oxford University Press (*The Mirror and the Lamp* by M. H. Abrams); Laurence Pollinger and the Estate of the Late Mrs Frieda Lawrence (*The Complete Poems of D. H. Lawrence, The Collected Letters of D. H. Lawrence, The Rainbow* and *The Plumed Serpent* by D. H. Lawrence); Prentice-Hall Inc. (*Literature and the Irrational* by Wayne Shumaker); Princeton University Press (*The Collected Works of C. G. Jung*); Routledge & Kegan Paul Ltd (*The Collected Works of C. G. Jung*); University of California Press (*Counter Statement* by Kenneth Burke); The Viking Press Inc. (*The Complete Poems of D. H. Lawrence* and *The Rainbow*); A. P. Watt & Son (*Collected Poems of W. B. Yeats*); Yale University Press (*The Philosophy of Symbolic Forms* by Ernst Cassirer).

General Editor's Preface

This volume is one of a series of short studies, each dealing with a single key item, or a group of two or three key items, in our critical vocabulary. The purpose of the series differs from that served by the standard glossaries of literary terms. Many terms are adequately defined for the needs of students by the brief entries in these glossaries, and such terms will not be the subjects of studies in the present series. But there are other terms which cannot be made familiar by means of compact definitions. Students need to grow accustomed to them through simple and straightforward but reasonably full discussions of them. The purpose of this series is to provide such discussions.

Some of the terms in question refer to literary movements (e.g. 'Romanticism', 'Aestheticism', etc.), others to literary kinds (e.g. 'Comedy', 'Epic', etc.), and still others to stylistic features (e.g. 'Irony', 'The Conceit', etc.). Because of this diversity of subject-matter, no attempt has been made to impose a uniform pattern upon the studies. But all authors have tried to provide as full illustrative quotation as possible, to make reference whenever appropriate to more than one literature, and to compose their studies in such a way as to guide readers towards the short bibliographies in which they have made suggestions for further reading.

John D. Jump

University of Manchester

'*Nous les pouvons donq bien appeller barbares, eu esgard aux regles de la raison, mais non pas eu esgard à nous, qui les surpassons en toute sorte de barbarie.*'

Montaigne

'*I can scarcely imagine that there is any spectacle more interesting and worthy of reflection, than one of these unbroken savages.*'

Darwin

'*O dass wir unsere Urahnen wären.*
Ein Klümpchen Schleim in einem warmen Moor.'

Gottfried Benn

Introduction

The nostalgia of civilized man for a return to a primitive or pre-civilized condition is as old it seems as his civilized capacity for self-reflection. And it is a familiar characteristic of human nature that almost every step towards what would generally be regarded as increased sophistication or progress is accompanied by misgivings frequently leading in turn to doubts about the whole enterprise of civilization. It must be recognized at the outset, then, that the term primitivism properly refers to a dauntingly ancient and universal human characteristic with a correspondingly wide range of manifestations. I emphasize this since any attempt to chart the meaning of this term must, as it seems to me, proceed with a healthy respect for its natural untidiness. As soon, at least, as we pass beyond the recognition of a familiar nostalgia to consider its specific manifestations in literature and the history of thought it becomes difficult to see the wood for the variety as well as the sheer abundance of the trees.

One helpful way of imposing order on the uses of this term is that adopted by Arthur O. Lovejoy and George Boas in *A Documentary History of Primitivism and Related Ideas in Antiquity*. The operative word in this title is 'ideas' for the authors base their compendious historical survey on a division of the term 'primitivism' into its logical possibilities. 'Primitivism', for example, is opposed to 'anti-primitivism' (Lovejoy and Boas, *passim*); 'hard' to 'soft' primitivism (ibid. pp. 9–11); and 'cultural' to 'chronological' primitivism (ibid. pp. 1–11). For the authors' purpose in recording and clarifying a chapter in the history of ideas this, as it were, spatial organization of the topic into a logical cartography is admirably appropriate. I propose, however, to do something different, if not indeed exactly contrary. Without wishing to ignore the historical aspect, I wish to consider some of the specifically critical problems raised by the literature for which this term is commonly used. It seems to me that rather than a logical cartography of the idea of primitivism the critical reader wishes to have a sense of the quality and kind of imaginative creation to which this idea or impulse has given rise. Hence, where Lovejoy and Boas are concerned with abstracting central concepts from their literary and philosophical material, my interest will be very largely in indicating the problems of making such abstractions outside of the specific imaginative and moral worlds of the works in question. Although 'primitivism', particularly in political and philosophical writing, quite properly denotes an idea or complex of ideas in the Lovejoy and Boas sense, this makes it only the more important to remember that within the world of a poem or a novel the primitivist feeling and even an apparently direct primitivist injunction has, or is likely to have, a carefully defined symbolic status. While the term may quite properly cover both an idea and a poetic symbol, then, this study is concerned with the latter; with the sense in which it 'must not mean, but be'. In practical terms this means for example, that a figure like Rousseau, who is important in the history of primitivism generally, will be of less importance to the present discussion.[1]

Yet even in purely critical contexts the term is not used with any obvious consistency, or even with a generally recognized attempt at such. It tends in fact to appear as a nonce usage, each critic assuming its general meaning to be apparent enough and going on to make his own precise reference clear in context. James Baird, for example, in a comprehensive study of primitivism in Melville and other late nineteenth-century writers (see *Ishmael*, p. 25), virtually

[1] Cf Fairchild, *The Noble Savage*, pp. 120–39, for a useful general account of Rousseau's relation to primitivist literature and thought.

excludes from his general definition such an important figure as
D. H. Lawrence whom M. H. Abrams has cited as a representative
twentieth-century primitivist (*A Glossary of Literary Terms*, New
York, rev. ed. 1971, p. 138). No doubt any attempt to find a
common aesthetic principle in all the writers who could be discussed under this heading would lead to the conclusion suggested
by Robert Goldwater in *Primitivism in Modern Art* (p. xxiv) that
there are as many different definitions of the term as there are
artists answering to this general description. And this casual usage
is not necessarily a bad thing; particularly since it reflects the fact
that the term 'primitivism' refers primarily to a basic human feeling
and does not denote a conscious or cohesive movement even to the
limited extent that the French Symbolists or the English Romantic
poets might be said to constitute one. We cannot refer to 'the
Primitivists' as we do, for example, to 'the Romantics'. Ludwig
Wittgenstein's comment on the problem of definition seems peculiarly appropriate to the present instance: 'Many words in this sense
then don't have a strict meaning. But this is not a defect. To think
this would be like saying that the light of my reading lamp is no
real light at all because it has no sharp boundary.' (*The Blue and
Brown Books*, Oxford, 1958, p. 27.) Literary definitions have a way
of being in some sense true without necessarily being very helpful
and the first necessity in the present instance, it seems to me, is to
insist on the inappropriateness of imposing a too rigid theoretical
structure on this topic whether historically, logically or otherwise.

Yet having said this we can still very usefully investigate in the
spirit of Wittgenstein's lamp image that loose affiliation of meanings implied by critics' use of the same term in relation to very
different writers. Indeed, it is these very differences that make such
an investigation potentially illuminating and C. G. Jung has a
caveat on the interpretation of dreams, which suggests a procedure
for dealing with such differences in a systematic and illuminating

way. If we compare Jung's 'dream' to the primitivist material and his 'conscious situation' to the artistic context then the following comment indicates a way of coping with the radical relativity of meaning that we encounter in the use of primitive motifs: 'I would even assert that without knowledge of the conscious situation the dream can never be interpreted with any degree of certainty. Only in the light of this knowledge is it possible to make out whether the unconscious content carries a plus or a minus sign.'[1] This study proceeds by a similarly pragmatic attention to specific cases. My intention is not to devise a comprehensive single meaning for this wide-ranging term but rather to bring out in the very range of its possible applications the basic critical questions which will illuminate individual works. While primitivism itself is not a constant entity its different forms can be approached with the same initial questions. As in Jung's case, what seems to be required is not so much a definition as a methodology.

And it is because I wish in this spirit to chase into the open some of the basic critical, and indeed moral, problems of primitivism that the emphasis of this study falls on works written in the nineteenth and twentieth centuries in which, as it seems to me, these problems are raised in the most complex and interesting way, yet which, unlike the earlier forms, have received little systematic critical attention. For reasons to be discussed more fully in Chapter 3, this modern primitivism differs crucially from such earlier manifestations as the ancient myth of the golden age; the renaissance and eighteenth-century interest in the noble savage that lies behind Rousseau;[2] and the traditional dichotomies between art and nature or town and country. As this generalized enumeration itself perhaps suggests, these earlier primitivist conventions derive much

[1] *The Collected Works of C. G. Jung*, ed. G. Adler, M. Fordham, H. Read, trans. R. F. C. Hull, vol. 16 © 1954, 1966 by Bollingen Foundation), New York, p. 154.

[2] For Rousseau's relation to earlier traditions of the Noble Savage, cf. Chinard, *L'Amerique et le Reve Exotique*, Paris, 1913.

of their poetic point from their very conventionality. They are most typically used as the imaginative *donnée* that frames an obviously stylized view of human experience. As Frank Kermode points out in his very relevant essay on *The Tempest*,[1] even though a factual account of Bermuda savages is part of its source material, the actual imaginative mode of *The Tempest* is pastoral drama. The literal anthropological material, in other words, is subsumed into a traditional stylization of experience. While any given work in such a tradition, as in the case of *The Tempest*, will have its own kind of complexity, its primary *donnée* is to assume a simplifying remove from the texture of common experience. We accept the primitivist element in it as part of a working hypothesis. A practical example of this distinction is H. N. Fairchild's suggestion of an inconsistency on Dr Johnson's part in attacking the idea of the noble savage in conversation yet using it uncritically in a moral essay (*The Noble Savage*, p. 336). This seems to me an indication rather of Johnson's recognition that the noble savage *is* a convention and cannot be taken literally at its face value. But the works of modern primitivism considered in this study are different in this major respect that their primitivist material does not typically fall into an established convention of stylization. In a work such as *Heart of Darkness*, for example, the exploration and moral assessment of the primitivist experience or the primitive self treats the whole issue much more literally and in doing so subjects the whole idea of the primitive to a more radical scrutiny. The meaning and value of the primitivist urge is now itself the central issue and it is explored in such a way as to genuinely disturb civilized responses and assumptions in a way that is not typical of the established literary conventions. For *Heart of Darkness* such categories as 'primitivist' and 'anti-primitivist' are meaningless and such modern works, which in themselves comprise an inward exploration of the primitivist impulse, provide a rich ground for

[1] *The Tempest*, ed. Frank Kermode (London, 1964), p. lxi.

examining the problems of primitivist motifs and feeling in literature generally.

The form of the following discussion, then, reflects the foregoing considerations. Rather than beginning with a comprehensive definition I take a number of works that have in different ways invited the term 'primitivist' and consider them in the light of the same question: what kind of moral value and imaginative life has the primitivist element in this particular instance? As a pragmatic focus for this I suggest two broad categories reflecting the important polarity that seems to me to emerge from such comparisons: the first comprising those writers who attempt to actually recreate the mentality or sensibility of primitive man as it were from the inside, and the second category comprising those who in some way use the primitive motif more externally as an idea or metaphor. This bald distinction indicates only the extremes of the scale and will require considerable clarification and modification in the course of discussion, but it is, I think, a helpful way of indicating the kind of discriminations in imaginative mode in terms of which the primitivist element can most usefully be defined. At this point, however, it seems best to proceed to some specific illustrations.

I

Primitive Sensibility

I use the term primitive, or mythic, sensibility to refer to the recreation of what many anthropologists have believed to be the most essential qualities of pre-civilized feeling and thought. Since our entire knowledge of early forms of mental life is necessarily inferential and has never been a matter on which all authorities have agreed, the question of its anthropological validity, an important and tricky issue, will have to be considered in more detail later. For the present, however, I will simply indicate those tendencies of feeling and thought whose appearance in works of literature has led to comparison with some of the influential, if not always reliable, anthropological accounts of the primitive world view.

Perhaps the most important point in an anthropological account of primitive man is that mythic sensibility refers to a *way* of feeling and thought, not to specific ideas or mental *objects*. We are concerned here not with the mythical objects or stories themselves but with the primary mode of response to the external world and to human nature from which all the particular mythic forms derive. This distinction is of considerable importance since mythic sensibility not only implies therefore the most radical qualities of primitive mental life but in literature something of this ancient mode of thought and feeling can be recreated without necessary recourse to actual primitive objects or beliefs. A writer, in short, may evoke the ancient response to life without being overtly or even consciously primitivist.

The fundamental characteristic of primitive sensibility from which its other features can logically be derived is the absence,

B

from a modern scientific standpoint at least, of a firm and rational distinction between the inner world of feeling and the external order of existence. Ernst Cassirer, who sums up some central tendencies of twentieth-century anthropological thought, puts it as follows:

> The linguistic term 'polysynthetic' has indeed been applied to the mythical imagination, and the term has been explained as meaning that for the mythical imagination there is no separation of a total complex into its elements, but that only a single undivided totality is represented – a totality in which there has been no 'dissociation' of the separate factors of objective perception and subjective feeling.
>
> (*The Philosophy of Symbolic Forms*, II, pp. 45–6)

The implication of this is that primitive man in effect projects the needs and desires of his own nature as objective qualities of the external world. In Cassirer's words:

> Accordingly, the world of mythical ideas, precisely in its first and most immediate forms, appears closely bound up with the world of efficacy. Here lies the core of the magical world view, which is saturated with this atmosphere of efficacy, which is indeed nothing more than a translation and transposition of the world of subjective emotions and drives into a sensuous, objective existence.
>
> (p. 157)

One of the most pervasive manifestations of this radical subjectivism of mythic consciousness is primitive animism. To the animistic mentality the external world is pervaded by spirits or powers, sometimes known collectively as 'mana'; the projection from our point of view of human desires and fears. All attempts to describe this mode of consciousness are bedevilled by the necessity of using modern terminology for a mental world which did not know the distinctions or share the assumptions that such terminology inevitably tends to imply. The mistranslation of the North American Indian term Manitou as 'Great Spirit' is a classic exemplification of civilized man's distortion of the mythic sense by the imposition of what seems the nearest available term. Where the modern term 'spirit' generally implies a transcendent supernatural dimension, mythic consciousness appears not to have known our long-standing dichotomy of spiritual and material. 'Mana' is not an independent spiritual entity so much as an inherent quality of the concrete objects of the environment and yet it provides the focus for attitudes that we can only describe as religious. Primitive man apparently felt in all aspects of the natural world, such as weather, animals and vegetation, the manifestation of a will and a mentality somehow comparable to his own. While no doubt feeling his environment as frequently hostile, primitive man none the less felt his relation to it as continuous rather than radically transcendent or alien. An insight into the primitive relationship with the natural environment is given in Cassirer's account of the 'momentary god'.

Here we have the mythico-religious proto-phenomenon which Usener has sought to fix with the term 'momentary god'. 'In absolute immediacy,' he says, 'the individual phenomenon is deified, without the intervention of even the most rudimentary class concept; that one thing which you see before you, that and nothing else is the god.' (p. 280) To this day, the life of primitive races shows us certain features in which this process is almost tangibly clear. We may recall examples of it which Spieth adduces: water found by a thirsty person, a termite mound that hides and saves someone, any new object that inspires a man with a sudden terror – all these are transformed directly into gods. Spieth summarizes his observations with the words: 'To the mind of the Evé, the moment in which an object or any striking attributes of it enter into any noticeable relation, pleasant or unpleasant, with the life of man, that moment a Trõ is born in his consciousness.' It is as though the isolated occurrence of an impression, its separation from the totality of ordinary, commonplace experience produced not only a tremendous intensification, but also the highest degree of *condensation* and as though by virtue of this

> condensation the objective form of the god were created so that it veritably burst forth from the experience.[1]

This passage emphasizes the radical subjectivity of this world view and catches the primitive disregard for a settled and separate supernatural order as the focus of its strong religious instinct.

Given such a world view it is natural that primitive man should attempt to come to terms with his environment not through scientific mastery but by appealing to the animistic powers. Elaborate propitiatory observances are to be found, for example, among many primitive peoples when killing their principal means of subsistence, or even their enemies. And this applies not just to the killing of men or even animals, such as bears and whales, but can apply equally to the felling of trees. This relation to the natural environment, spanning a range of feeling from grateful worship to superstitious terror, can be broadly summed up as natural, or cosmic, piety; a term for which two observations are especially relevant for present purposes. Firstly the powers of nature, just as they do not correspond to the Christian supernatural, are not to be seen as morally 'good' or beneficent in anything like a Christian sense. The primitive awe is as closely allied to terror as to worship and the natural deities to which it gives rise are as little amenable to moral pressure almost as nature itself. 'Mana' is felt as a curious cross between a conscious being and a natural phenomenon like an electric charge. As Frazer points out, the ritual associated with such powers is as much like the literal and scientific practice of insulating an electrical charge as symbolic or religious observance. Indeed it has even been suggested that the sense of 'mana' originated in the experience of static electricity.[2] Natural piety, therefore, does not denote a view of the universe as good so much as an unquestioning submission to its ways.

[1] *Language and Myth*, trans. Susanne K. Langer (New York, Dover Publications Inc., 1946), pp. 33–4. Reprinted through permission of the publisher.
[2] C. R. Aldrich, *Primitive Mind and Modern Civilization* (New York, 1931), p. 42.

The second observation follows from this. Since natural piety is not essentially a moral concept it does not militate against bloodshed, or even cannibalism, as our civilized ethical systems, however ineffectively at times, may be said to do. Where we think of conduct in more personal and creative terms as moral responsibility or an effort of self-determination, primitive man thinks in terms of taboos expressing a superstitious awe of the potencies of external nature. Taboo is a way of coming to terms with the mysterious and the ungovernable which still leaves them beyond comprehension or control and therefore accepts the state of things as essentially unchanging. The propitiatory observances of warriors and huntsmen are not expressive of any desire to behave otherwise but only to avoid the possible consequences of offending the natural powers or the spirits of the departed. Fortunately, however, a detailed study of taboo practices and their possible interpretations is not necessary for the present discussion. These remarks are simply intended to indicate that natural piety, whatever its precise manifestations and meaning in primitive life, is a complex of feeling that resists definition in either the religious or the moral terms to which it seems most closely akin in our civilization. It is a mode of feeling and thought that is profoundly at one with the natural world, that accepts human life as part of that world, and therefore does not question the moral propriety of the cosmic order. It does not, or cannot, adopt that kind of philosophic detachment.

For present purposes, then, the three most important features of the primitive world view are animism, natural piety, and the rituals through which they are expressed. Although they obviously have considerable residual life the first two of these particularly have lost their potency in Western civilization as dominant modes of assimilating and ordering experience. They all, however, reappear in certain works of literature in such a way that the inadequacy of religious, moral or psychological formulation to the mode of feeling that is recreated has led critics to draw anthropological parallels.

Two major, yet very different, writers for whom such comparisons have been made are D. H. Lawrence and Herman Melville. A consideration of both, therefore, can show very different ways in which these ancient modes of response can be evoked in modern English. We may consider Lawrence first.

For this purpose it is best to leave, for a while at least, Lawrence's overtly primitivistic works such as his Mexican and American fiction, for some of the best examples of his recreation of the mythic response to life are to be found in my opinion in such works as *The Rainbow* and some of the short stories set in England. And these works have the added advantage for present purposes that this mode of response can be illustrated more clearly without the further factor of an overtly primitivist intent. Several critics have observed that Lawrence's exploration of the emotional life frequently evokes a level of feeling and a response to the external world that recreate essential aspects of the mythic world view.[1] The following passage, for example, occurs early in *The Rainbow* as Lydia Lensky begins to recover from the total emptiness that has followed the death of her husband and her settling in England. After the virtual extinction of her former personality, a process of psychic rebirth takes place starting at a very instinctual level beyond her conscious recognition or understanding. To render this, Lawrence re-establishes the most elemental relatedness between Lydia and the world around her; he reawakes in her that animistic awe by which the individual and his world are made deeply at one.

She was sent to Yorkshire, to nurse an old rector in his rectory by the sea. This was the first shake of the kaleidoscope that brought in front of her eyes something she must see. It hurt her brain, the open country and the moors. It hurt her and hurt her. Yet it forced itself

[1] Cf. especially Mary Freeman, *D. H. Lawrence: A Basic Study of his Ideas* (New York, 1955), p. 233; E. Goodheart, *The Utopian Vision of D. H. Lawrence* (Chicago, 1963), p. 59; Mark Spilka, *The Love Ethic of D. H. Lawrence* (Indiana, 1955), pp. 12–16.

upon her as something living, it roused some potency of childhood in her, it had some relation to her.

There was green and silver and blue in the air about her now. And there was a strange insistence of light from the sea, to which she must attend. Primroses glimmered around, many of them, and she stooped to the disturbing influence near her feet, she even picked one or two flowers, faintly remembering in the new colour of life, what had been. All the day long, as she sat at the upper window, the light came off the sea, constantly, without refusal, till it seemed to bear her away, and the noise of the sea created a drowsiness in her, a relaxation like sleep. Her automatic consciousness gave way a little, she stumbled sometimes, she had a poignant, momentary vision of her living child, that hurt her unspeakably. Her soul roused to attention.

Very strange was the constant glitter of the sea unsheathed in heaven, very warm and sweet the graveyard, in a nook of the hill catching the sunshine and holding it as one holds a bee between the palms of the hands, when it is benumbed. Grey grass and lichens and a little church, and snowdrops among coarse grass, and a cupful of incredibly warm sunshine.

She was troubled in spirit. Hearing the rushing of the beck away down under the trees, she was startled, and wondered what it was. Walking down, she found the bluebells around her glowing like a presence among the trees.

(London, Heinemann, 1955, pp. 47–8)

This is a beautiful and characteristic passage. In a basically simple, direct prose that is yet constantly shot through with odd images or turns of phrase Lawrence follows the movement from total dejection to a peculiar emotional culmination. By the end of the passage the hints of a strange 'otherness' in the description of the sea, sky and flowers have gathered in the experience of the bluebells glowing 'like a presence' among the trees. In this final moment there is the vivid suggestion of an unspecified being or power immanent in the woodland surroundings. The delicacy of the phrase 'like a presence' is that it conveys this impression without any explicit hypostatization or personification. It does not enforce a consciously focused image, but simply evokes a feeling. By this troubling indeterminacy of reference the phrase invites the reader to project into it the suggestiveness of the entire passage; it makes him re-enact the emotional projection that suddenly surprises the character herself. The overall effect is that her emotional state is simply felt in the environment as an apparently objective characteristic; a mysterious 'presence' among the trees.

Such effects are not, of course, peculiar to Lawrence, they are familiar in romantic literature generally, but he is an especially illuminating example in view of the relation of this, as we shall see, to his later overt primitivism, for it is apparent that this episode concerning Lydia Lensky is an inward recreation of an animistic response that closely parallels the experience of the 'momentary god' as described by Cassirer. This is true not only of the final effect but of the way the whole episode is structured to prepare for it. The sudden transfiguration of the outer world of nature by the inner world of feeling is the culmination of an increasing fusion of the two throughout; the environment is assimilated by the woman with growing intimacy as she progressively opens herself towards it. In the opening paragraph the environment is totally external and can be felt only as a hurtful, alien pressure. By the third paragraph, however, the sun's rays that were hurting her eyes have begun to suffuse her body with warmth. The shift from sight to touch suggests an absorption of the outer world that continues in the final paragraph with the shift to the sense of hearing. She is actively attending now rather than merely reacting mechanically to its insistence. From the passiveness of the opening verb in 'She was sent to Yorkshire . . .' she moves to an active seeking out of the experience in the final moment among the bluebells: 'Walking down, she found the bluebells. . . .'

Even granted the general structure of the episode it is apparent that its peculiar conviction, as has already been suggested, is an effect of Lawrence's characteristic language. In recreating something of an ancient mode of feeling Lawrence, in this novel at least, does not attempt to reject or deny the civilized mentality. He rather, by subtle and continual displacements of normal usage, feels back as it were through the mental patterns of modern English towards a less rationally developed kind of consciousness. His use of the word 'presence' here, his exerting pressure on it to make it yield something beyond its normal meaning, is entirely typical. He leans on words forcing them to extend their area of meaning yet without obvious wrenching from their 'normal' sense. The repetition of 'hurt' (in 'It hurt her brain, the open country and the moors. It hurt her and hurt her.') has a comparable effect. Without apparent departure from a simple and direct English Lawrence, like Wordsworth, imparts a special aura to such key words throughout his prose. The general effect is to create over the whole work a subtly unstated aura of feeling around the apparently literal description. It is in this characteristic aura that Lawrence's mythic and animistic sensibility finds expression.

It is of course difficult to demonstrate such effects satisfactorily in a short passage since their imaginative force derives from the cumulative recreation of a world view in the novel at large and the same applies to other primitivist features. Since once again, however, these features will reappear in other primitivist contexts it is worth noting how they are manifest in *The Rainbow*. For example, both anthropologists and primitivist writers have emphasized the radically different sense of time in a world of primitive subjectivity. Once again Cassirer (*The Philosophy of Symbolic Forms*, II) provides a useful summary:

> The fact is that long before the human consciousness forms its first concepts concerning the basic objective differentiations of number, time and space, it seems to acquire the subtlest sensitivity to the peculiar periodicity and rhythm of human life.
>
> (p. 108)

Thus we see that for mythical consciousness and feeling a kind of biological time, a rhythmic ebb and flow of life, precedes the intuition of a properly cosmic time.

(p. 109)

The essential point is that time is conceived in its psychological aspect, that is to say, as it impinges on the individual's possibly varying state of mind, rather than as a fixed and objective category. And even in the present brief passage can be seen something of the subjective indeterminacy, from a more modern, intellectual point of view, that characterizes the portrayal of time in *The Rainbow*. Several critics have remarked on Lawrence's insistent use of a narrative device that is not uncommon in the novel but which is rarely used so extensively or with quite this effect.[1] Lawrence plays on an ambiguity of verbal tense by which a simple preterite form covering both particular and habitual actions enables him to treat of quite disparate units of time as if they were a homogeneous continuum. In the present passage, for example, the time span implied at different points in the narrative varies from generalized states lasting perhaps for several months to the experience of a few moments as among the bluebells. Apart from the dramatic compression and the control of narrative perspective that this makes possible, its further effect in Lawrence's case is to displace unobtrusively the more usual sense of time as an objective chronology. The effect of this in *The Rainbow* is that the sense of time is conveyed as an aspect of the movement of feeling, of the cyclic and rhythmic processes of life. It recaptures that 'subtlest sensitivity to the peculiar periodicity and rhythm of human life' of which Cassirer speaks. The whole world of *The Rainbow* is one in which the sense of fixed, objective time is delicately and unobtrusively undermined.

The Rainbow also exemplifies another Lawrencean feature which

[1] Cf. especially Roger Sale, 'Narrative technique in *The Rainbow*', *MFS*, V (1959), 29–38.

provides a fruitful comparison with other primitivist writers. The sense of the emotional life as a movement of elemental and impersonal forces lends to many events that are on the face of it quite commonplace, a distinctly ritualistic feel. Tom Brangwen's preparations before going to propose to Lydia Lensky are a case in point. Again a lengthy quotation seems necessary to catch the spirit of the episode.

One evening in March, when the wind was roaring outside, came the moment to ask her. He had sat with his hands before him, leaning to the fire. And as he watched the fire, he knew almost without thinking that he was going this evening.

'Have you got a clean shirt?' he asked Tilly.

'You know you've got clean shirts,' she said.

'Ay – bring me a white one.'

Tilly brought down one of the linen shirts he had inherited from his father, putting it before him to air at the fire. She loved him with a dumb, aching love as he sat leaning with his arms on his knees, still and absorbed, unaware of her. Lately a quivering inclination to cry had come over her, when she did anything for him in his presence. Now her hands trembled as she spread the shirt. He was never shouting and teasing now. The deep stillness there was in the house made her tremble.

He went to wash himself. Queer little breaks of consciousness seemed to rise and burst like bubbles out of the depths of his stillness.

'It's got to be done,' he said as he stooped to take the shirt out of the fender, 'it's got to be done, so why balk it?' And as he combed his hair before the mirror on the wall, he retorted to himself, superficially: 'The woman's not speechless dumb. She's not cluttering at the nipple. She's got the right to please herself, and displease whosoever she likes.'

This streak of common sense carried him a little further.

'Did you want anythink?' asked Tilly, suddenly appearing, having heard him speak. She stood watching him comb his fair beard. His eyes were calm and uninterrupted.

'Ay,' he said. 'Where have you put the scissors?'

She brought them to him, and stood watching as, chin forward, he trimmed his beard.

'Don't go an' crop yourself as if you was at a shearing contest,' she said anxiously. He blew the fine-curled hair quickly off his lips.

He put on all his clean clothes, folded his stock carefully, and donned his best coat. Then, being ready, as grey twilight was falling, he went across the orchard to gather the daffodils.

(The Rainbow, pp. 36–7)

There is nothing in Tom's actions that immediately resembles the rituals by which primitive peoples celebrate, and indeed from their point of view make possible, important developments of the individual's life such as the passage from childhood to maturity. Yet there is much in his manner and attitude that imparts a similar significance to his actions. He calls for a clean, white shirt 'inherited from his father'; washes; trims his beard and picks some daffodils. These actions are performed almost automatically as the apparently inevitable order of preparation even while with another part of his mind he is still weighing up the merits of his decision. Meanwhile the servant Tilly, forced into the role almost of acolyte, highlights the profound change that has come over his personality: 'Now her hands trembled as she spread the shirt. He was never shouting and teasing now. The deep stillness there was in the house made her tremble.' At this moment of crisis in his psychological development Tom instinctively adopts traditional forms by which to give the inner event an objective expression and by doing so to bring it securely into being. One feels it is all more for his own sake than for hers. When the time arrives the traditional forms carry his immediate fears and indecision before them. This is one of Lawrence's unique abilities. Without straining a simple domestic scene he can invest it with a feeling and give it a psychological function for which primitive ritual seems the nearest analogy. Comparable episodes occur elsewhere in the novel, frequently with different handling in detail, of course, and sometimes with more overtly primitivist overtones such as when the pregnant Anna dances before the Lord. One of the finest of such ritual scenes in Lawrence occurs at the end of his play *The Widowing of Mrs Holroyd*. While the dead miner's wife and mother are washing his naked body, the younger woman's emotions concerning her dead husband suffer a profound change as she undergoes the inner change from wife to widow. Once again the literal domestic necessity acquires the sense of a ritual or inner necessity and a perfectly natural action is imbued with a level of feeling beyond the character's apparent resources in everyday life.

Without explicit statement or overt departure from the assumptions of a later world view, Lawrence animates his whole narration with qualities of what many anthropologists have designated as the life feeling of an older mode of consciousness. Hence although the overall direction of the work is not atavistic, nor would one wish to make any such claim for this passage considered in isolation, anthropological formulations such as Cassirer's do seem to illuminate that suffusive mode of feeling and response that gives *The Rainbow*, and so much of Lawrence, its distinct tone. F. R. Leavis speaks of the 'distinctive vibration' of *The Rainbow* and of Lawrence's profound 'reverence' for life. The 'vibration' is very much that of an intuitively animistic sensibility and if one had any quarrel with the word 'reverence' it would be only that its overtones are rather too spiritual; more appropriate perhaps to George Eliot. Although Lawrence makes considerable use of religious language and symbolism, it just as frequently appears in connection with characters who have lost this primitive at-oneness with the natural world. The term 'natural piety' rather than the language of religion catches the elemental and unreflecting awe from which Lawrence's characteristic attitude seems to derive.

The foregoing remarks are not exhaustive but suggest the manner in which primitive modes of feeling pervade a work like *The Rainbow* even though it has few overtly primitivist motifs and is anything but atavistic in its overall values. The novel attempts to gather into a modern sensibility some of the richness and strength of the primitive sensibility without surrendering the poise of the civilized self. In rendering the emotional density of the Brangwens' inner lives, particularly at moments of crisis, Lawrence has an apparently spontaneous recourse to those modes of feeling and thought by which many anthropologists have believed primitive man to have ordered his experience, the prominent features of which are animism, natural piety and ritual.

Another major writer whose work shows qualities of feeling and response comparable to those attributed by anthropologists to primitive man is Herman Melville. As might be expected, Lawrence was an admirer of Melville and in fact wrote one of the first critical studies of his work. Yet the manner in which this primitivist element appears in Melville is very different from what we have seen in Lawrence and provides a useful basis for comparison.

Firstly the genesis of the primitive feeling seems to have been rather different in each case. Relatively little is known of Melville's imaginative life before he began to write but his first works, *Typee* and *Omoo*, published when he was twenty-seven and twenty-eight respectively, arise from his experience of being kept as the increasingly suspicious and unwilling guest of a tribe of Polynesian cannibals. So that whereas Lawrence, as is apparent from biographical and internal evidence, always had the intuitive relation to the natural world that has been outlined above, Melville it seems was suddenly presented with actual primitives; *Typee* and *Omoo* representing his first moral and imaginative assimilation of this experience. Lawrence, as we shall see, seems to have derived his later primitivism largely from reflection on the nature of his own sensibility, while Melville's seems to have been externally objectified for him at an early stage. However, as James Baird points out in his comprehensive study of primitivism in Melville, the really interesting result of this Polynesian experience is its re-emergence in a modified and more suffusive form as part of the complex symbolism and feeling of *Moby Dick*. Melville's assimilation of the experience has awakened an inward sympathy for the primitive world view such that it is assimilated as a spontaneous attribute of his own sensibility.

But something of the difference of development in this regard can be felt in the work itself. Melville's confrontation with the primitive occurred when his mind was already alive to the kind of moral, philosophic and religious issues that were to concern him for the rest of his life: when, that is, the world of ideas was supremely important to him. His initial use of the primitive experience is not unnaturally therefore as a philosophic and moral idea. In *Mardi*, written between *Omoo* and *Moby Dick*, the use of the Pacific experience is in a more discursive than novelistic context. And even in *Moby Dick* the primitive is given an intellectual or philosophic role to play that is quite different from the unobtrusive pervasiveness of this element in *The Rainbow*.

Given Melville's different way of assimilating the primitive experience it is not surprising that, as the emphasis of Baird's study suggests, the primitivist element in *Moby Dick* should be principally a matter of the choice of symbolic material. And so primitivist motifs such as the practices of carving and tattooing, the figure of the 'wise old savage', the custom of sworn friendship or *Tayo*, the myth of the great sea-beast, and the special significance of the colour white, are all transposed from their original contexts in Polynesian and Oriental cultures into the symbolic pattern of Moby Dick. Yet, as Baird points out, something of the feeling that invests these beliefs and practices in their primitive cultural context is part of their effective symbolic life in the novel (*Ishmael*, p. 6). The assimilation of these primitive motifs, even though it is put to conscious symbolic use, has been accompanied by a reawakening of the primitive life feeling from which they derive.

In order to illustrate precisely what this means in terms of the novel, it is as well to remark first on the different strategy of dramatization in *Moby Dick* as compared to *The Rainbow*. Indeed, as we shall see in other instances too, the narrative strategy is often a key factor in defining the meaning, or status, of the primitive motif. The technical difference that *Moby Dick* is narrated by Ishmael himself while *The Rainbow* is in the third person reflects the different presentation of the world views implied in each novel. In Lawrence's case, although something of his earlier attempt to write the novel in the first person can still be felt in his close identification with the central characters, the kind of effects that we have seen to be vital to both the passages quoted depend very much on the author's rendering of states of feeling that the characters themselves could not articulate and of which they are generally not fully conscious. Lydia, for example, is just awakening from her trance-like indifference and Lawrence catches the state still antecedent to her arousal. His art in such episodes is to so by-pass the most conscious and social personality of the character as to suggest further resources of feeling and response. Although the character's world view exhibits a romantic subjectivity in the sense already elaborated, it is dramatized by the author from a standpoint outside the consciousness of the character himself. It is Lawrence's use of his own voice that points up the unreflecting subjectivity of Lydia.

In *Moby Dick*, on the other hand, the whole experience comes through the mind of the highly self-conscious narrator, Ishmael, who habitually wrests from each detail of his life some general significance in the world of ideas. In this novel in fact we find not so much a direct dramatization of mythic consciousness as a study of the inadequacy of an opposite world view, that of the rational and civilized mind, as a total human response to life. Ishmael, an outsider to normal human society as his biblical name implies, is caught between the limited extremes of the harpooner Queequeg and Captain Ahab and hence provides the theatre of consciousness within which the conflict between these two world views can be joined. Ahab represents an extreme Faustian commitment to an individualist and questioning use of the intellect, to deeply rooted or instinctive assumptions that Ishmael as a scion of Western civilization cannot help but share in some measure, while Quee-queg's unquestioning cosmic submission exemplifies a totally different mode of response.

Some such brutally schematic observation seems necessary to indicate the general deployment of primitive motifs in *Moby Dick* but the greatness of the novel is, of course, that it makes such general remarks peculiarly thankless and a specific illustration is clearly required to show how these different world views are typically weighed against each other in the novel using the consciousness of Ishmael to hold them in simultaneous focus. The episode of the giant squid provides a brief example. The lookout has just sighted a white mass in the distance which he takes to be the white whale. Without pausing to question this assumption Ahab orders the launching of the whale boats.

The four boats were soon on the water; Ahab's in advance, and all swiftly pulling towards their prey. Soon it went down, and while, with oars suspended, we were awaiting its reappearance, lo! in the same spot where it sank, once more it slowly rose. Almost forgetting for the moment all thoughts of Moby Dick, we now gazed at the most wondrous phenomenon which the secret seas have hitherto revealed to mankind. A vast pulpy mass, furlongs in length and breadth, of a glancing cream-colour, lay floating on the water, innumerable long arms radiating from its centre, and curling and twisting like a nest of anacondas, as if blindly to clutch at any hapless object within reach. No perceptible face or front did it have; no conceivable token of either sensation or instinct; but undulated there on the billows, an unearthly, formless, chance-like apparition of life.

As with a low sucking sound it slowly disappeared again, Starbuck, still gazing at the agitated waters where it had sunk, with a wild voice exclaimed – 'Almost rather had I seen Moby Dick and fought him, than to have seen thee, thou white ghost!'

'What was it, sir?' said Flask.

'The great live squid, which, they say, few whale ships ever beheld, and returned to their ports to tell of it.'

But Ahab said nothing; turning his boat, he sailed back to the vessel; the rest as silently following.

Whatever superstitions the sperm whalemen in general have connected with the sight of this object, certain it is, that a glimpse of it being so very unusual, that circumstance has gone far to invest it with portentousness. So rarely is it beheld, that though one and all of them declare it to be the largest animated thing in the ocean, yet very few of them have any but the most vague ideas concerning its true nature and form; notwithstanding they believe it to furnish to the sperm whale his only food. For though other species of whales find their food above water, and may be seen by man in the act of feeding, the Spermaceti whale obtains his whole food in unknown zones below the surface; and only by inference is it that any one can tell of what precisely, that food consists. At times, when closely pursued, he will disgorge what are supposed to be the detached arms of the squid; some of them thus exhibited exceeding twenty and thirty feet in length. They fancy that the monster to which these arms belonged ordinarily clings by them to the bed of the ocean; and that the Sperm whale, unlike other species, is supplied with teeth in order to attack and tear it.

There seems some grounds to imagine that the great Kraken of Bishop Pontoppodan may ultimately resolve itself into squid. The manner in which the bishop describes it, as alternately rising and sinking, with some other particulars he narrates, in all this the two correspond. But much abatement is necessary with respect to the incredible bulk he assigns it.

By some naturalists who have vaguely heard rumors of the mysterious creature here spoken of, it is included among the class of cuttle-fish, to which, indeed, in certain external respects it would seem to belong, but only as the Anak of the tribe.[1]

Neither Ahab nor Queequeg plays any significant role in this particular episode but the polarity of attitudes for which they

[1] *Moby Dick* by Herman Melville. Norton Critical Edition, edited by Harrison Hayford and Hershel Parker. © 1967 by W. W. Norton & Co. Inc. New York, the publisher. pp. 237-8.

provide the principal focus in the novel is suggestively portrayed. The two extremes appear here in the seamen's response to the squid as this is seen in the light of Ishmael's further reflections. Dramatically a heightened response to the squid is prepared for by the narrative strategy of allowing the reader, despite one or two misgivings, to share the seamen's initial assumption that the creature is in fact a whale. This throws an eerie and perplexing light on the subsequent description as the details progressively belie this assumption yet without immediately resolving themselves into an explicable alternative. The initial sense of mystery and awe created by this narrative perspective is then if anything intensified by Ishmael's attempt in the remainder of the passage to explain the 'wondrous phenomenon' rationally in terms of natural history. And it is from this point that two different kinds of response to the creature are superimposed and thereby mutually highlighted. From the first awed reaction of the sailors a dual process is at work: Ishmael's account concentrates on known facts and rational inferences concerning the creature while the imaginative movement generated by the sailors' awed surprise moves from personification, through superstition, to fable. Starbuck's address to the squid leads to an account of whaler's superstitions generally and finally to the fabulous 'great Kraken'. And it is a moot point which response emerges as either the stronger or the more appropriate. Ishmael's persistent rationalism is obliged to encompass not only the creature itself but also the superstitious response it almost universally commands. In the very process of explaining or containing it rationally Ishmael testifies to the almost universal power of spontaneous superstition in the face of such a phenomenon. The brief final paragraph beautifully reiterates the imaginative movement of the whole passage. A 'naturalist's' theory is tentatively suggested and apparently endorsed by Ishmael yet in the final words the creature again slips the noose of scientific classification and escapes back into the world of primitive fable.

The superstitious awe of the sailors is again reminiscent of Cassirer's description of the 'momentary god', and the way in which this primitive response manifests itself in defiance of the mental habits of practical science is typical of the attitude to Moby Dick and his kin throughout the novel. It seems that these nineteenth-century mariners seeking primeval beasts in their own natural element have perforce awakened in them something of primitive man's superstitious awe. Even the necessity of the hunt does not contradict or diminish this feeling. The difference in Ahab's attitude, for example, is not that he hunts but that he does not share or refuses to acknowledge this natural piety. And to the extent that he does feel the pull of it his resentful hatred is only inflamed. For the primitive man on the other hand we have seen that even the hunted or dead beast does not cease to command a superstitious fear and respect.

Despite its discursive and philosophic bias, then, *Moby Dick* effects an inward recreation of the old animistic awe, Queequeg and the White Whale providing centres around which this response can focus, while Ishmael's relationship with Queequeg and his part in the chase give him an unusual access to it. And the different stylistic medium of *Moby Dick*, its more discursive mode, is an important aspect of the kind of dramatization in question. Whereas Lawrence recreates dramatically a sense of 'unknown modes of being' without generally allowing this to come into conscious focus either for the character or the reader as an unusual experience, Ishmael's insistence on rational understanding takes him consciously to the limits of such understanding whereupon, in situations of elemental fear and wonder, the primitive world of superstition and animistic projection comes suddenly to life. In Lawrence such a response is assimilated unquestioningly into the texture of experience. It is the difference between the unobtrusive indirection of Lawrence's phrase '*like* a presence' and Starbuck's directly superstitious apostrophe 'thou white ghost!'.

It is difficult to determine quite what technical anthropological appreciation if any Melville had of the similarity between the mythic and animistic dimension he imparted to *Moby Dick*, particularly in the figure of the White Whale itself, and the life of primitive man; but of his intuitive recognition of the similarity there is no doubt. Newton Arvin quotes in this connection Melville's own remark: 'Your true whale-hunter is as much a savage as an Iroquois. I myself am a savage.' And Arvin goes on:

> Certainly in his half-fearful, half-worshipful attitude toward the Sperm Whale he was closer to the primitive than to the civilized mind; and he gives us his own clues to this when he identifies the Whale with the dragons of Perseus and St George, or recalls that the Hindu god Vishnu was incarnate in a whale. Yet he probably did not know, literally, that for many primitive peoples – for peoples as remote from one another as the Annamese, the Tongans, and the Unalit Eskimos – the whale is, or once was, the object of a solemn cult, a sacred animal as truly as the cow or the bear was elsewhere. He probably had not heard that some of these peoples prepared themselves for a whale-hunt by fasting for days beforehand, by bathing themselves repeatedly, and by other rites; that some of them, after a whale's life had been taken, propitiated his ghost by holding a communal festival; and that others when a dead whale was washed ashore, accorded it a solemn burial and preserved its bones in a small pagoda by the sea.[1]

That it is so difficult to determine quite how much technical knowledge and conscious intention went into the creation of these very tangible effects testifies to the intuitive and thoroughly inward manner of Melville's recreation of primitive consciousness. The complex of feeling surrounding the white whale is more than a literary man's annexation of exotic material, it is an awakening in Melville of the animistic and mythic sensibility on his own account and in his own terms.

Again the foregoing comments on *Moby Dick* are not intended

[1] *Herman Melville* (New York, William Morrow & Co. Inc, 1950), pp. 185–6.

to be exhaustive but to suggest what is meant by primitive sensibility in Melville and how it relates to the work as a whole. We may round off this section with a consideration of one last feature of primitive life attested by anthropologists and manifest in several primitivist writers. In both of these works by Melville and Lawrence there are attitudes to death significantly different from the more usual attitudes of our civilization. Melville's Queequeg provides the most striking instance.

Queequeg's unquestioning cosmic acceptance seems to give him an extraordinarily impersonal sense of his own existence. He not only, like the other savages aboard the *Pequod*, Tashtego and Daggoo, performs quite impassively the most dangerous of the everyday tasks of whaling but he leaps with apparently foolhardy courage into situations such as diving to rescue a shipmate from the sinking head of a whale. Yet when he is mysteriously convinced that his own death is upon him, without any evidence of illness or special danger, this same impersonal acceptance paradoxically allows him to face it, and indeed prepare for it, with unshakeable equanimity. His death, like so many of the difficult moments of his life, has its proper and sustaining ritual. He has a coffin made and lies calmly waiting to die. Baird (*Ishmael*, p. 245) quotes anthropological authority for this, to most of us, remarkable characteristic of many primitives peoples that they seem untroubled and unaffected by the imminent prospect of death when they feel that their natural life cycle is completed. Such an attitude to death throws the polarity between Ahab and Queequeg into its sharpest relief since death is at once the final ignominy of the human situation for the man resentful of his helpless submission to the conditions of existence and by the same token it provides the ultimate manifestation of natural piety.

Lawrence's works are pervaded by a similar attitude to death which can be seen already in *The Rainbow*. In the early part of the novel, for example, where the bond of cosmic acceptance is strongest, Lawrence recounts with parenthetic brevity the death of Tom Brangwen's father: 'When he was seventeen, his father fell from a stack and broke his neck.' After this unceremonious despatching of a figure who has been given considerable attention in the preceding pages, Lawrence goes on to describe the family's adjustment to the sudden loss. The routine necessities of farming life assert themselves and the violent occurrence finds its level, quite unsentimentally, as part of the continuing process of life. The later death of Tom Brangwen himself, who is drowned in a swirling, black flood, has its even more vitalistic overtones. In this latter instance, however, more attention is given to the grief of the surviving members of the family which highlights the very different reaction of the educated and rationalist older son, Tom. He alone is unable to accept his father's death: 'He could never forgive the Unknown this murder of his father.' (*The Rainbow*, p. 250.) The abhorrence of death in this absolute and principled way is a symptom for Lawrence of civilized estrangement from the life process; the loosening of the bond of natural piety. It is reminiscent of Ahab's resentment of the whale that has taken his leg.

Lawrence has left an especially moving testament to his own natural piety in the matter of death. Dying slowly of tuberculosis and in circumstances of extreme bitterness he seems in some measure none the less to have welcomed the opportunity of facing his death knowingly and with acceptance. The poem *The Ship of Death* on which he was still working as he died is perhaps his most impressive and beautiful achievement in the primitivist spirit. Although death is used in the poem with a wider reference than his own personal fate, his use of the Etruscan funeral ritual of burying in the tombs of the dead a small boat supplied with provisions clearly expresses Lawrence's own ready anticipation of what he considered the last major human experience. The image is informed throughout with a calm and unforced trust that has little in common with either religious faith or stoical resignation. The poem needs to be read in full but the following lines indicate its tone.

> A little ship with oars and food
> and little dishes, and all accoutrements
> fitting and ready for the departing soul.
>
> Now launch the small ship, now as the body dies
> and life departs, launch out, the fragile soul
> in the fragile ship of courage, the ark of faith
> with its store of food and little cooking pans
> and change of clothes,
> upon the flood's black waste
> upon the waters of the end
> upon the sea of death, where still we sail
> darkly, for we cannot steer, and have no port.[1]

Lawrence's sense of death as continuous with life rather than the mere negation of it is substantiated by the simple but moving concern for the domestic details of dishes and cooking pans. Just as Lawrence elsewhere gives a ritual dimension to domestic life so here the primitive ritual is brought poignantly to life by the domestic literalism. Again the primitive feeling blends totally with the texture of everyday life.

This is perhaps the best note on which to end these remarks on primitive sensibility in Lawrence and Melville. Neither of the novels considered in detail is primitivist in the sense of urging a regression to earlier human states. Although Ahab, for example, is seen in a critical perspective he is also a tragic and Promethean figure and the issue we have been pursuing is only one strand in the inexhaustible suggestiveness of *Moby Dick*. The present concern is simply to show how such works are pervaded with qualities

[1] *The Complete Poems of D. H. Lawrence*, 2 vols, ed. V. de Sola Pinto and F. W. Roberts (New York, 1964), pp. 718–19.

of feeling for which anthropologists' descriptions of primitive life provide the nearest comparison. The primitive affinity is made in large measure explicit in *Moby Dick* itself and is made retrospectively so for *The Rainbow* by the nature of Lawrence's later and more deliberate primitivism. This, however, brings us to the discussion of conscious primitivism.

2

Conscious Primitivism

In the foregoing discussion of mythic consciousness I have suggested strains of feeling without which the symbolic structure of *The Rainbow* or *Moby Dick* would lose its conviction and point. Using the discussion of these works as a point of comparison we may go on to consider what is probably the more common use of primitive material in literature, the conscious reference to primitive motifs in which the main point or effect is not the inward recreation of ancient modes of feeling but the moral or symbolic use to which such references can be put. This means in effect that such primitivism of its nature can only be self-conscious. The spontaneous recreation of mythic sensibility and the deliberate use of primitive motifs are not, of course, incompatible, as some of the examples in the previous chapter amply demonstrate. It seems, however, that where the pendulum swings completely from an inward recreation to an external reference the potential meaning and the imaginative status of the primitive motif are radically modified. This difference of course, does not imply a value judgement: it suggests only that self-conscious primitive reference generally enters into or creates a very different imaginative world from those considered so far.

Ironically enough the force of this distinction emerges most clearly from a comparison with one of Lawrence's less successful endeavours in conscious primitivism. *The Plumed Serpent*, published early in 1926, was written some ten years after *The Rainbow* when Lawrence, having suffered considerable artistic and social estrangement within his own country, had lost much of the spontaneity and optimism of the period between his marriage in 1912 and the outbreak of the war. Despite its frequent brilliance in detail this later novel is generally, and I think rightly, considered to be an artistic failure and a full investigation of the critical and moral problems it raises need not concern us now. Our present interest lies in the way in which the primitivism of *The Plumed Serpent* parallels more self-consciously, if less successfully, the features of mythic sensibility that inform *The Rainbow*. It is as if the later novel were a desperate attempt to recapture by an effort of will the spontaneously mythic world view of the earlier one. The following passage shows the kind of critical problems involved.

The world was different, different. The drums seemed to leave the air soft and vulnerable, as if it were alive. Above all, no clang of metal upon metal, during the moments of change.

> 'Metal for resistance.
> Drums for the beating heart.
> The heart ceases not.'

This was one of Ramón's little verses.

Strange, the change that was taking place in the world. Always the air had a softer, more velvety silence, it seemed alive. And there were no hours. Dawn and noon and sunset, mid-morning, or the up-slope middle, and mid-afternoon, or the downslope middle, this was the day, with the watches of the night. They began to call the four watches of the day the watch of the rabbit, the watch of the hawk, the watch of the turkey-buzzard and the watch of the deer. And the four quarters of the night were the watch of the frog, the watch of the fire-fly, the watch of the fish, the watch of the squirrel.

'I shall come for you,' wrote Cipriano to her, 'when the deer is thrusting his last foot towards the forest.'

That meant, she knew, in the last quarter of the hours of the deer; something after five o'clock.

It was as if, from Ramón and Cipriano, from Jamiltepec and the lake region, a new world was unfolding, unrolling, as softly and subtly as twilight falling and removing the clutter of day. It was a soft, twilight newness slowly spreading and penetrating the world, even into the cities. Now, even in the cities the blue *serapes* of Quetzalcoatl were seen, and the drums were heard at the Hours, casting a strange mesh of twilight over the clash of bells and the clash of traffic. Even in the capital the big drums rolled again, and men, even men in city clothes, would stand still with uplifted faces and arms upstretched, listening for the noon-verse, which they knew in their hearts, and trying not to hear the clash of metal.

> 'Metal for resistance.
> Drums for the beating heart.'

(London, Heinemann, 1955, pp. 356–7)

In discussing the earlier passage from *The Rainbow*, I commented on Lydia's subjective transformation of the external world by the unwitting projection of her psychological state. The present passage ostensibly deals with something comparable, the transformation of the external world experienced by the devotees of the pagan religious revival. But the actual impression made by this passage is very different. And the basic difference is that the new sense of the world emanating from Ramón and Cipriano is referred to directly as an objective fact rather than being felt simply as an inherent quality of the evoked scene. Indeed, unlike Lydia's case, the present passage goes so far as to suggest that this transformation is perceptible even to an outside observer. Furthermore, whereas in *The Rainbow* passage the whole presentation of the environment was informed with Lydia's emotional response, here there is little in the environment that takes on the feel of subjective emotional life. Rather the reverse. The objectification of this emotional projection as 'casting a strange mesh of twilight over the clash of bells and the clash of traffic' focuses a dichotomy in which the basic disparity between the inner and the outer emerges only the more clearly and irreconcilably. Rather than a recreation of the ancient life feeling we have a mere assertion of the intended effect with the result that we are made only the more aware of how foreign it is to our habitual assumptions.

The closest approach in this passage to an animistic relation with the environment is in the mention of the air left by the drums with a new softness 'as if it were alive' and until 'it seemed alive'. Lawrence's ability to render the sensory and psychological effect of light and sound is unsurpassed but in this instance the very awareness that this is a sensory effect of the drums militates against the word 'alive' acquiring an animistic aura comparable to the 'presence' of the bluebell passage. And although in the passage just quoted Lawrence is not forcing an animistic sense from the description, it is made obvious elsewhere by Ramón himself that this is the intended basis of his pagan religious feeling:

> 'The earth is alive. But he is very big, and we are very small, smaller than dust. But he is very big in his life, and sometimes he is angry. *These people, smaller than dust,* he says, *they stamp on me and say I am dead. Even to their asses they speak, and shout Harreh! Burro! But to me they speak no word. Therefore I will turn against them, like a woman who, lies angry with her man in bed, and eats away his spirit with her anger, turning her back to him.*'
>
> (p. 194)

This is an extreme instance of the difference between inward recreation and external assertion. The author makes this at best vulnerable material explicit in the mouth of a character who in turn attributes it to a clumsy personification of the earth. It is in the highest degree self-conscious. The weakness of the primitivist endeavour in *The Plumed Serpent* lies in the gap between this explicitly asserted belief in the animation of the cosmos and the actual presentation of natural life which, however sensitive and brilliant in other ways, does not undercut a civilized world view to make available the primitive oneness and awe.

It is natural therefore that the cosmic piety of Ramón and his followers should have an equally imposed or factitious quality about it. Of course Lawrence, and indeed Ramón, are aware that this pagan religious feeling is being imposed on an initially recalcitrant environment but even so it has not the conviction it requires and the main point here is that such conscious assertion has now become the primary method rather than the recreation for the reader of the characters' own sense of moving always within the orbit of natural piety. It is interesting, too, that in this novel Lawrence sets up quasi-religious rituals as an inverse parallel to Christian observances.[1] The present passage, for example, is reminiscent of the Angelus bell observance in certain catholic countries. Compare that with the following sentences from *The Rainbow*:

> Two miles away, a church-tower stood on the hill, the houses of the little country town climbing assiduously up to it. Whenever one of the Brangwens in the fields lifted his head from his work, he saw the church-tower at Ilkeston in the empty sky. So that as he turned again to the horizontal land, he was aware of something standing above him and beyond him in the distance.

(p. 1)

Without any overt subversion of the Christian implications these sentences provide a closer introduction to the ancient life feeling than the deliberate subversion of Christian ritual in *The Plumed Serpent*. The principal respect in which *The Plumed Serpent* feels successfully towards ritual form is in the gradual change in the heroine, Kate Leslie. Jascha Kessler has pointed out how the effects on her of the Quetzalcoatl cult are pointed up by details suggesting 'rites de passage' such as when she crosses Lake Sayula.[2] In the overall effect, however, the presentation of a primitive religious sense remains factitious and external.

[1] Cf. James C. Cowan, 'The symbolic structure of *The Plumed Serpent*', *Tulane Studies in English*, XIV (1965), 75–96.
[2] Cf. Jascha Kessler, 'Descent into darkness: The myth of *The Plumed Serpent*', in *A D. H. Lawrence Miscellany*, ed. Harry T. Moore (London, 1961), pp. 239–61.

We may round off these remarks on *The Plumed Serpent* with a consideration of its dramatization of the sense of time. In the present passage Ramón and Cipriano have supplanted the precision of clock time with a quasi-primitive system following the changing cycle of day and night. This theme recurs frequently in *The Plumed Serpent* with an intended significance that the following sentences make explicit:

> Stir in the air, everybody enjoying those periodical shivers of fear! But for these shivers, everything much the same as usual. The church remained shut up, and dumb. The clock didn't go. Time suddenly fell off, the days walked naked and timeless, in the old, uncounted manner of the past. The strange, old, uncounted, unregistered, unreckoning days of the ancient heathen world.
>
> (p. 285)

Once again, although there is an immediate dramatic efficacy about the detail of the stopped clock, it is hardly adequate as a psychological recreation of the 'ancient heathen world'. And in the passage we have been considering the institution of a pseudo-primitive analogue of clock time only highlights by contrast the normal social use that is in fact being made of it. It apparently differs from clock time only in that it enables the Mexican to be as amiably imprecise about making appointments as he generally is about keeping them. Whereas in *The Rainbow* a pervasive indeterminacy of narrative tense allows time to assert itself in purely psychological terms through the cycles of generations, the change of seasons and the daily routine of farming life which collectively comprise the structure of the novel, in *The Plumed Serpent* the action follows an almost touristic itinerary lasting only several months in a country with a relatively minimal variation in the seasons. The sense of cosmic rhythm that informs *The Rainbow* is stuck as an empty idea on Kate Leslie's experiences in Mexico.

The striking impression that emerges from the detailed parallels between these two novels is that in the later one Lawrence is in effect trying by a highly self-conscious effort of will to recreate a mode of feeling that was once spontaneously and in large measure unreflectingly his. In this later exercise in primitivism Lawrence seems to be forcing or working against the best qualities of his own sensibility. And the important point here is not just that the primitivism is self-conscious for we have already seen that this can be successful in *The Ship of Death*. It is rather that knowledge of primitive life is being used simply externally instead of informed with imaginative life.

However, if such an external use of primitivist motifs is unfortunate in Lawrence this is not necessarily the case for other writers; particularly when their own sensibility or attitude to the primitive is very different from his. The failure of *The Plumed Serpent* in this respect is that it unjustifiably assumes its treatment of the primitive to have included an inward imaginative recreation. We may now consider several writers whose use of primitive motifs is successfully external because the implied standpoint from which they treat it is firmly and consistently so.

Joseph Conrad's *Heart of Darkness* is an illuminating instance particularly in comparison with *The Plumed Serpent*. Conrad's whole sense of the primitive is, of course, quite different from Lawrence's. Where Lawrence sees it as expanding and enriching the individual emotional life with a cosmic dimension and a new psychological profundity, Conrad sees the necessary isolation, cosmic and human, of the primitivist hero Kurtz. Such general differences, however, derive from the basic fact of Conrad's conceiving the whole experience from within the stand-point of a moral civilization. He sees it in terms of a release from civilized moral restraint which derives its potentially heroic aspect in two ways: by comparison with the moral hollowness of contemporary civilized man and by virtue of the courage, albeit perverse courage, that is required to pursue this human potentiality to its extreme. But the very implication that such courage is required highlights the fundamental assumptions that the primitivist urge, if indulged, can only lead to the destruction of the civilized self and that such an eventuality is necessarily evil. Although Lawrence's attitude to the primitive varied from a Utopian faith to the sober awareness that we can no longer 'cluster at the drum'[1] he is always sympathetic in the same measure as his rejection of contemporary civilization was radical and bitter. Conrad's criticism of social and political life is from within the moral assumptions of western civilization and he views the primitive, whatever its fascination and relevance for civilized man, as an undesirable extreme.

And once again we find that this difference finds expression in the radical narrative conception of the works in question. Kate Leslie, who provides the theatre of consciousness for *The Plumed Serpent*, is placed in a position of immediate and absolute choice between the civilized and the primitive; she is invited to join the pantheon of Mexican deities and to marry one of the leaders of the revival movement. It is true, of course, that she in large measure resists making this choice and indeed the interest of the novel depends largely on the shifts and qualifications in her position. Yet the fact remains that a decision is forced on her in face of the actual social and personal consequences of a real-life primitive commitment. Lawrence is clearly exploring the possibility of a literal social application of the primitivist impulse. Conrad, on the other hand, presents the primitivist urge through the narrator, Marlowe, who is not only recollecting 'in tranquillity' the whole experience but who in fact has only had that experience at second hand as an imaginative reconstruction on his part of Kurtz's final years. The narrative structure, in other words, focuses attention on the problem of Marlowe's response to Kurtz when the latter is already safely dead. The only practical moral decision forced on Marlowe is of

[1] *Phoenix: The Posthumous Papers of D. H. Lawrence*, ed. E. D. McDonald (London, 1936), p. 99.

D

what to say to Kurtz's former fiancée. By catching Marlowe between the dead Kurtz and the living woman Conrad's narrative strategy sets up the crucial distinction between action and the more problematic realm of imaginative sympathy and yet still forces the problem urgently upon him. Kenneth Burke's remarks on Gide make a similar point with characteristic acuteness.

> I do not believe that his work can be evaluated properly unless we go beyond the subject-matter to the underlying principles. His choice of material even implies a certain obscurantism, assuming a sophistication on the part of the reader whereby the reader would not attempt too slavishly to become the acting disciple of his author's speculations. Surely Gide would be the first to admit that we could not build a very convenient society out of Lafcadios, however admirable they are. I should take the specific events in Gide as hardly more than symbols: their parallel in life would not be the enacting of similar events, but the exercising of the complex state of mind which arises from the contemplation of such events with sympathy.
>
> (*Counter-Statement*, New York, 1931, p. 104)

The narrative strategy of *Heart of Darkness* embodies a similar distinction by which the original Kurtz is essentially the catalyst for the creation in Marlowe's mind of an imaginative symbol for a moral truth. It constructs a qualifying context within which to contain its primitivist sympathy as opposed to the open ended structure of *The Plumed Serpent* which does everything to force a direct confrontation with social reality. Conrad has, of course, opposite weaknesses to Lawrence as well. Where Lawrence's very literalism and boldness are the frequent source of profound insights, Conrad's reserve betokens some unwillingness to follow out the full implications of his material. His account of Kurtz's actual behaviour, the 'unspeakable rites', remains highly elliptical and deserves E. M. Forster's well-known comment applied by F. R. Leavis to *Heart of Darkness* that Conrad '... is misty in the middle as well as at the edges, that the secret casket of his genius contains a vapour rather than a jewel; and that we need not try to write him down philosophically because there is, in this particular direction, nothing to write.' (*Abinger Harvest*, London, 1936, p. 135.) However, this weakness in Conrad's case of surreptitiously lightening the moral load, so to speak, of his novel is secondary to the larger attempt to maintain the delicate distinction between literal action and imaginative sympathy. And particularly in conjunction with a work like *The Plumed Serpent* it provides a representative case for the basic dilemma of primitivist literature. Primitivism in the sense of the promotion of a return to a pre-civilized way of life is always in danger of bad faith in that the primitivist urge can never actually be realized or tested in real life and is likely therefore to be nothing more than a safely civilized indulgence, an easy assumption of moral superiority. Yet the dilemma has its genuine aspect. Dissatisfaction with civilized existence or a narrow mode of inner life can be so radical as to demand this drastically different alternative while at the same time the very recognition of this need is itself knowingly the product of civilized self-reflection. Within the narrative structure of the tale Conrad's Marlowe, that indefatigable connoisseur of moral nuance, holds this irresolvable duality in focus. With Lawrence, though few people familiar with the man and his *œuvre* would now support the once frequent charge of fascism, it is often difficult to determine precisely what kind of imaginative status should be accorded to his primitivist injunctions. Even if one does not agree with them such charges are readily comprehensible in the light of *The Plumed Serpent*. However, the larger interest of this comparison for present purposes is to highlight what the two works have in common.

In general we may say that, whereas in *The Rainbow* and *Moby Dick* we could sense the authors feeling towards a mode of sensibility which would blend the strengths of the primitive and the civilized, in the present cases the primitive appears in its more purely alien aspect; Lawrence destructively promoting a rejection of civilization for the primitive and Conrad concerned to find the proper attitude for the completely civilized man to adopt towards the primitive as a human potentiality. Yet in both cases its significance lies in its being held within a conscious and civilized frame of reference by which it is therefore seen as an alien alternative; and it presents itself in each case not as simply part of the novel's created world view but as a conscious issue or problem. This is the feature that characterizes all the uses of primitive motifs considered in the present chapter: that they assume a world view or frame of consciousness within which the primitive experience, with whatever sympathy or distaste, is viewed as an abnormal phenomenon.

T. S. Eliot is a clear instance of this. Eliot's relevance here lies not simply in his well known use of anthropological motifs in *The Wasteland* but also in his articulate awareness of the cultural situation that gives rise to such a phenomenon. His review of Joyce's *Ulysses* emphasizes the importance of myth as a way of ordering the apparent chaos of contemporary life.

> In using myth, in manipulating a continuous parallel between contemporaneity and antiquity, Mr Joyce is pursuing a method which others must pursue after him. They will not be imitators any more than the scientist who uses the discoveries of an Einstein in pursuing his own, independent, further investigations. It is simply a way of controlling, of ordering, of giving a shape and a significance to the immense panorama of futility and anarchy which is contemporary history.
>
> *(Dial, LXXV (1923), 483)*

The interest in myth here bears a clear family relation to Eliot's theory of the 'dissociation of sensibility', the long influential theory of cultural disintegration which also involved a projection of cultural superiority on to the past yet was essentially a way of defining what he felt to be wrong with the present. It is hardly surprising then that in *The Wasteland*, his own most ambitious expression of contemporary disintegration, Eliot should have used as his centre of moral reference primitive myths and rituals as outlined by Sir James Frazer and Jessie Weston. Indeed, the present passage might be seen as his prospective self-justification for following Joyce's lead in that poem. Yet the very terms of this review make the quality of his general interest in such material plain. It is reminiscent of Thomas Mann's statement in his lecture on Freud that myth is the earliest stage in the life of the race and the latest in that of the individual (*Adel des Geistes*, Stockholm, 1945, p. 592). Where the primitive thinks in unwittingly mythic terms the fully civilized man can turn to mythic forms with a sophisticated awareness of their peculiar ontological status. And so Eliot turns to myth, in effect, as to a highly civilized cultural acquisition.

In *The Wasteland* Eliot uses the myth of the Fisher King and its medieval avatar, the Grail Legend, as a metaphorical framework placing the contemporary experience in a satiric and pitiful perspective. Indeed this, as it were, tactical use of the primitivist motif to provide a poetic focus on the present has the effect of emphasizing the incongruity between contemporary and primitive life. It is at the furthest possible remove from the recreation of mythic sensibility considered in the previous chapter. The typical effect is that seen in these lines:

> While I was fishing in the dull canal
> On a winter evening round behind the gashouse[1]

or

> That corpse you planted last year in your garden,
> Has it begun to sprout? Will it bloom this year?[2]

[1] *The Complete Poems and Plays of T. S. Eliot* (New York, 1952), p. 43.
[2] Ibid., p. 39.

The grotesque incongruity of these rererences to the Fisher King and the buried god, deliberately bathetic in the one case and nightmarish in the next, highlights the alien remoteness of the ancient mode of life. As Douglas Bush puts it, the 'mythological allusions are magical (though far from meaningless) incantations in a frame of irony.'[1] Although Eliot's use of the primitive here is highly honorific, therefore, it is so only in a tactical sense and does not denote a Lawrencean trust in pre-civilized and instinctual modes of feeling and thought. Far from promoting such a return Eliot desiderates a reinvigoration of the European cultural and religious order which is to our civilization what these myths were to primitive man. His actual nostalgia is for the 'inexplicable splendour' of the high points of our civilization. Eliot's use of the primitive is essentially academic and is in fact derived entirely at second hand from anthropological studies. As his own notes to *The Wasteland* make clear, it is only one element in the sophisticated cultural eclecticism of the poem's network of allusions.

Something of Eliot's response to any more literal primitivism, his horror of reductive irrationalism, is suggested by the lines in 'The Love Song of J. Alfred Prufrock':

> I should have been a pair of ragged claws
> Scuttling across the floors of silent seas.
>
> *(Complete Poems and Plays*, p. 5)

This nostalgia for a simpler existence is attributed only to the timorous Prufrock and the image itself is one of inverted Darwinism, a pure and horrifying regression to one of the lowest forms of animal life.

Eliot's interest in ritual form is worth mentioning in this connection too. Eliot's attitude to contemporary life seems to contain a large element of distaste and, given his later conversion to High

[1] *Mythology and the Romantic Tradition in English Poetry* (Cambridge, Mass., 1937), p. 511.

Church Christianity, it is not surprising that his subsequent use of ritual forms should have an otherworldly implication. In *Murder in the Cathedral* and *Ash Wednesday* the ritual suggests a spiritual dimension standing over and beyond everyday life rather than an inherent characteristic of the natural world such as we have seen in Lawrence. For Eliot both myth and ritual are forms seen by the lights of culture and faith respectively over and against the messiness of everyday life, whereas for Lawrence they are simply part of the full human response to the natural world. Although both men were concerned with what they felt to be the psychic disintegration and emotional barrenness of their time, Eliot looked on myth more intellectually as a principle by which complexity can be ordered and emotional meaning therefore restored while Lawrence felt the presence of the mythic world view rather as a psychological state, a deep emotional fullness, in which such disintegrative complexity is dissolved. Where Lawrence's primitivism comes from his own animistic sensibility, Eliot's primitivist motifs are derived from a highly developed cultural and religious tradition.

As I have already suggested, another major writer whose use of the ancient past is comparable to Eliot's is James Joyce. With Joyce, of course, we are already moving rather outside the scope of the present study since his major myths, the Ulysses and Daedalus stories, are literary rather than anthropological in their immediate origin. They do, however, address themselves to a similar function of lending form to the apparent chaos of personal and contemporary life. In *Ulysses*, Joyce, like Eliot, uses myth as a structural principle and a metaphorical medium to place the more literal action in a special perspective and again it comprises only one element in a sophisticated pattern of allusion spanning the whole of European culture and beyond.

Yet despite this generalized similarity the effect in the work itself is very different. For one thing the mythical element is less salient. It is felt obliquely as a structural principle more than by direct reference and this reflects its different relation to the literal narrative of contemporary life. Despite the detached and frequently ironical perspective from which the characters and action are viewed, the overall effect in this case is not satiric or belittling. On the contrary their very ordinariness is raised to the highest level of interest. The Joycean myth, unlike Eliot's, does not clash satirically with the narrative action but suffuses it with a timeless dignity that seems finally appropriate to its central and universal human concerns. Where Eliot's myth leads towards the speaker's turning his back on the contemporary wasteland in the hopes of a spiritual resolution, Joyce's moves towards the comprehensive 'yes' that ends Molly Bloom's soliloquy.

Yet this fusion of the mythical and the literal, the ancient and the contemporary, remote as it is from Eliot, is still very different from Lawrence's infusion of a modern narrative with animistic feeling. Where Lawrence in a work like *The Rainbow* unobtrusively assimilates the civilized into the primitive sensibility, Joyce's highly self-conscious stylistic techniques maintain an awareness of the gap between past and present in order to present a multiple panorama of human history in a monumental act of consciousness. Joyce's *œuvre* may be seen as a celebration and pyrotechnical display of the developed human consciousness, and a conscious sense of historical and cultural distance is crucial to this effect. The ancient is one with the modern only as they are both seen to be gathered into this virtuoso performance of the human mind. The extraordinary *tour de force* in which Joyce describes the events surrounding the delivery of Mrs Purefoy's baby in a burlesque of literary styles running through the history of English literature is a case in point. The object to be celebrated is not simply the fact of birth and growth but the reverberation of the ideas of birth and growth in the human consciousness. Joyce's excursions, therefore, into the mythic past are quite different from the primitivist's atavistic rejection of the present. They are a journey for which the real point lies not in the supposed destination so much as in the mode of travelling; in the demonstrated power of the human consciousness.

In so far as Joyce's use of ancient myth is integral to a celebration of human life as transformed by the power of the human imagination, he invites comparison with W. B. Yeats. Yeats has been accredited with the first poetic use of *The Golden Bough*[1] and apart from this an eclectic use of mythological motifs from several ancient cultures pervades his work. Of course, Yeats as the writer of many short and occasional poems may be expected to respond less to generalization in this regard but the Yeatsian 'system' of *A Vision* gives considerable coherence to the *œvre*. And again the characteristic effect of such motifs is not to reject the present for the ancient past but to celebrate the timeless aspirations of the human spirit as embodied in myth and the products of the imagination. Although he has written some of the greatest poetry ever on political themes, the strong implication of the *œuvre* is that specific historical reality is ultimately of less importance than the timeless mythical forms to which it gives rise or the enduring human vitality it displays. A. O. Lovejoy has pointed out in a different context how cyclical theories of history can have a primitivist implication (Lovejoy and Boas, pp. 4–6, 79–84). Yeats's 'system' with its recurring historical 'gyres' makes for an imaginative commitment to a heroic past that tends to be bardic and celebratory rather than Utopian or corrective. It rehearses where we have been rather than suggest that we can or should return. Consider, for example, the opening and closing stanzas of 'Two Songs from a Play'.

> I saw a staring virgin stand
> Where holy Dionysus died,
> And tear the heart out of his side,
> And bear that beating heart away;

[1] John B. Vickery, '*The Golden Bough* and modern poetry', *Journal of Aesthetics and Art Criticism*, XV, 3 (1957), 274.

> And then did all the muses sing
> Of Magnus Annus at the spring,
> As though God's death were but a play.
>
> Everything that man esteems
> Endures a moment or a day.
> Love's pleasure drives his love away,
> The painter's brush consumes his dreams;
> The herald's cry, the soldier's tread
> Exhaust his glory and his might:
> Whatever flames upon the night
> Man's own resinous heart has fed.[1]

The sense of the human past evoked here includes a convincingly substantiated nobility and terror yet curiously blurs the historical focus. Its final effect is to bring an undefined mystery and grandeur to bear on the present. Yeats was a sympathetic admirer of Lawrence and his approving remarks on the now notorious conversations of Mellors and Connie Chatterley provide an insight into his own attitudes. His remark that the lovers speak a language 'ancient, humble and terrible' might more justly apply to the intention than the achievement of the novel but it suggests how for Yeats also the primitive terror and grandeur were not the exclusive prerogative of the ancient past. In Yeats, as in Joyce, an idea of the ancient past is used to give dignity to the present by suggesting an essential continuity.

Conrad, Eliot, Joyce and Yeats, then, four major modern writers, have all shown an interest in primitive life or ancient myth from the standpoint of their own civilization. The primitive motif is in each case very clearly contained within the civilized assumptions of the author as these are embodied in the imaginative context of the work. In conjunction with the earlier discussion of Melville and Lawrence the consideration of these four authors should indicate the different moral and imaginative worlds in which the recreation

---

[1] *The Collected Poems of W. B. Yeats* (2nd ed., London, 1950), pp. 239–40.

of mythic sensibility and the conscious use of primitive motifs are likely to occur. We have already seen, however, that these categories while providing a helpful polarity are not mutually exclusive and we may close this chapter with a consideration of a case in which this distinction, I think, is helpful precisely because it is less obvious than in the four preceding.

A work that may seem at first not to fit the category of an external use of primitive motifs is William Golding's *The Inheritors* (London, 1955), which is ostensibly set within the consciousness and sensibility of its primitive characters. Golding's narrative traces the supersession of a small group of Neanderthals by a group of creatures who are physically more developed, more sophisticated and more aggressive. The poignancy of the story derives from the presentation of each type both as they appear to themselves and as they appear to the others. The tale regrets the change but recognizes its inevitability; the new people, for example, have more mastery over their experience but this seems to imply their correspondingly larger scope for moral corruption. The whole effect, then, depends intimately on the ironies of point of view. Having followed the action entirely sympathetically through the less developed mentality of the earlier group, we suddenly see them quite impersonally in the penultimate chapter as merely pathetic and apparently subhuman creatures. Then in the final chapter the point of view shifts to the 'new people' who see their predecessors as 'red devils'. All the moral and dramatic life of the book therefore derives from the recreation from the inside of the more primitive sense of life to set against that of the slightly more advanced 'inheritors'.

If we consider the implied anthropological theory of the novel in the abstract, as opposed to the actual imaginative recreation of it, the presentation of the primitive world view in *The Inheritors* is comparable to much that we have seen in Lawrence. This world, for example, is animistic. Water that is flowing as opposed to

standing is 'awake'; as also the fire when it is lit. Spring is a manifestation of the female earth deity 'Oa' and its melting snows are
the water running from the belly of the 'ice-woman' on the
mountain tops. The exultant sensation of spring is expressed by
calling 'Oa' aloud and the initially negative reaction to the drunken
behaviour of the new people is the statement that 'Oa did not bring
them out of her belly'. And in keeping with this animistic response
to the natural world personal consciousness is in various ways
undeveloped while the body itself has a large degree of apparently
independent, almost intelligent, life. In other words human life is
still conducted at a very instinctual level. The sign, for example,
that the old man, Mal, is reaching his end is that he 'lifted his legs
like a man pulling them out of mud and his feet were no longer
clever'. And when more is required than an instinctual reaction, the
activity of thought is mainly habitual and communal. The old man,
Mal, keeps as it were the store of their collective thoughts and
when at the approach of his death he takes the unusual step of asking
them a question, it is with some surprise that they are recalled to
individual consciousness:

> One of the deep silences fell on them, that seemed so much more
> natural than speech, a timeless silence in which there were at first many
> minds in the overhang; and then perhaps no mind at all. So fully
> discounted was the roar of the water that the soft touch of the wind on
> the rocks became audible. Their ears as if endowed with separate life
> sorted the tangle of tiny sounds and accepted them, the sound of
> breathing, the sound of wet clay flaking and ashes falling in.
> Then Mal spoke with unusual diffidence.
> 'Is it cold?'
> Called back into their individual skulls they turned to him.
>
> (p. 34)

It is also noticeable in this passage that the mental state into which
they most naturally relax is not only a mindless silence but is also
timeless. Again the desire or capacity to organize experience objec-

tively in time is absent. Since their thinking consists entirely of timeless and unlocated 'pictures', it can only with great difficulty convey intellectual relations such as chronological order or cause and effect. The communication of mental concepts, the sharing of 'pictures', is therefore heavily dependent on the communal and habitual nature of their mental and sensory existence. Their inter-relations, like those of many Lawrence characters, depend on instinctual sympathies that by-pass centres of personal conscious-ness.

As a final feature we may mention the cosmic piety that Golding's primitives manifest in their attitude towards death. The grave of old Mal is dug in his presence while he is still alive and as he dies he is told 'softly':

'Oa is warm. Sleep.'

The movements of his body became spasmodic. His head rolled sideways on the old woman's breast and stayed there.

Nil began to keen. The sound filled the overhang, pulsed out across the water towards the island. The old woman lowered Mal on his side and folded his knees to his chest. She and Fa lifted him and lowered him into the hole. The old woman put his hands under his face and saw that his limbs lay low. She stood up and they saw no expression in her face. She went to a shelf of rock and chose one of the haunches of meat. She knelt and put it in the hole by his face.

'Eat, Mal, when you are hungry.'

She bade them follow her with her eyes. They went down to the river, leaving Liku with the little Oa. The old woman took handfuls of water and dipped their hands too. She came back and poured the water over Mal's face.

'Drink when you are thirsty.'

One by one the people trickled water over the grey, dead face. Each repeated the words. Lok was last, and as the water fell he was filled with a great feeling for Mal. He went back and got a second gift.

'Drink, Mal, when you are thirsty.'

The old woman took handfuls of earth and cast them on his head. Last of the people came Liku, timidly, and did as the others bid her.

Then she went back to the rock. At a sign from the old woman, Lok began to sweep the pyramid of earth into the hole. It fell with a soft swishing sound and soon Mal was blurred out of shape. Lok pressed the earth down with his hands and feet. The old woman watched the shape alter and disappear expressionlessly. The earth rose and filled the hole, rose still until where Mal had been was a little mound in the overhang. There was still some left. Lok swept it away from the mound and then trampled the mound down as firmly as he could.

The old woman squatted down by the freshly stamped earth and waited till they were all looking at her.

She spoke:

'Oa has taken Mal into her body.'

(pp. 90–1)

It is clear from the nature of this ritual as well as the features already enumerated that some care has gone into recreating a primitive world in terms of an anthropological scheme. In fact, though, Golding does not give an inward recreation of the primitive such as we find in Lawrence and I think that this can be ascribed to other considerations than the admittedly important one that Lawrence is a much greater writer, for the peculiar art of this book is actually to avoid a psychologically convincing recreation of a primitive world. The imaginative standpoint of the novel is not in fact limited to its dominant narrative viewpoint and the shift of point of view in the final chapters is the more obvious structural expression of an implied duality of viewpoint throughout. The deliberately simple syntax, which expresses the minimally developed consciousness of the primitives, is always an obvious stylistic device. The actual quality of the prose is not only at a constant remove from the mentality and experience described but it is so in a way by which the reader can hardly fail to be affected. The very use of the word 'picture', for example, which is a staple of the narrative method, introduces what is in fact a highly sophisticated concept to dramatize the primitive simplicity. And the authorial voice frequently uses such expressions whose sophistication clashes with the world view described. The opening image of this sentence, for example: 'A sharply sculptured cloud moved away from the sun and the trees sifted chilly sunlight over their naked bodies' (p. 15). Whether or not this effect is entirely deliberate on Golding's part, there is a balance throughout of a poignantly inward sense of the primitive existence and an external view of it because one is always aware of the stylistic mechanisms.

The upshot of this is that Golding is in effect offering the story as essentially a fable. While using genuine, or at least recognizable, anthropological categories, he does so in such a way as to give his characters a clearly limited imaginative status. The mechanism of primitive sensibility consciously pointed up as an effect of style operates as a kind of *ad hoc* literary convention registering that the essential interest lies at a less immediate level. The psychological conviction of the characterization is extremely tenuous but as a fable of the human implications of progress it is brilliant and compelling. If the recreation of the primitive mind were more convincing in terms of psychological realism the tale might gain as an anthropological exercise while losing something of its more universal reference.

The underlying indirectness of Golding's dramatization of the primitive in what is at first sight the most direct recreation of the primitive in his works suggests the status of this motif elsewhere in his writing. *Lord of the Flies*, for example, gives something of the same standpoint more obviously. In this macabre reversal of the English public school optimism of R. M. Ballantyne's *The Coral Island*, Golding suggests the weakness of the civilized order *vis-à-vis* the unrecognized emotions of the savage lurking within it. Not only do the English schoolboys left alone on the island themselves regress to savages but the reason they are there in the first place is that the older generation is using the sophisticated technical achievements of civilization in the primitive conflict of war. Yet at the end civilization, with all its drawbacks, is the only note of hope and the primitive is viewed always from the standpoint of the civilized. *The Inheritors* and *Lord of the Flies* are fables making essentially symbolic use of their primitivist material.

Pincher Martin and *Free Fall*, while evincing Golding's characteristic narrative methods, give more play to the complexity of characterization we generally associate with the novel. And in these two works Golding explores in a different way his sense of the dark underside of civilized human nature. Both heroes are caught in an extreme situation such that their normal social personality is dislodged; much as the dislodging of a large stone will reveal scurrying insects. Sammy Mountjoy's childhood fear of the 'old woman' in the dark and Pincher Martin's recurrent thoughts of eating or being eaten suggest a moral underside comparable to that which *Lord of the Flies* presents in fable form. That these last three works are all based on the experience of the Second World War in which Golding himself served may suggest something of the origin of his sceptical attitude towards both the primitive and a civilization that claims to have passed beyond it. In general, Golding's use of the primitive, like Eliot's, is part of a critique of contemporary civilized man but it is not given the inward recreation of a feasibly assimilable alternative to our mode of consciousness or way of life that we have seen in Lawrence. In short, the primitive in Golding is put to conscious symbolic use. It is subservient to a moral idea.

This is the major distinction between the works considered in each of these chapters. The quality of experience I have denoted as mythic sensibility emerges in the work itself as an existential reality resisting translation into symbolic or philosophic terms. For conscious primitivism the importance lies precisely in the philosophic or symbolic use of the primitive material.

The foregoing account has covered a great deal of ground with little time for qualification or expansion. One point, however, should emerge clearly enough. Given the very different kinds of moral and imaginative worlds seen briefly in these two chapters it is apparent that any consideration of an author's attitude to the 'primitive' and any definition of what this term denotes must first take into account the imaginative status and function of the primitive material in question. Although Lawrence and Eliot, for example, have both been in some sense sympathetic to the primitive, Eliot's tactical symbolic use of such material is equally opposed to either Lawrence's literal injunctions or his successful recreation of the archaic life feeling.

3
The Historical Context

In the opening pages of this study I remarked that although primitivist nostalgia can be traced from the earliest records of civilized reflection, the nineteenth and twentieth centuries saw radical changes in its manifestations in imaginative literature. Traditional literary and moral reference to the golden age or the noble savage gives way to the more complex and varied uses of primitive motifs and the recreation of primitive feeling exemplified in the two preceding chapters. It now remains to suggest something of the general nature and causes of this development. I remarked at the outset that since literary primitivism has such widely different meanings, it is of little use to suggest a comprehensive definition, and similarly in so far as modern primitivism may be seen as only one aspect of a widespread twentieth-century anti-rationalism,[1] it would be impracticable to explore all its intellectual and historical relations. I propose, therefore, to concentrate on some major aspects of the cultural situation in which these works appeared and suggest something of the ways in which these influences have been assimilated. Rather than attempt a complete historical survey, I think it is important to make some discriminations concerning the nature and relevance of 'influence' in this context.

Three important cultural factors immediately suggest themselves. The first, from within the literary tradition itself, is the relationship of primitivism to the romantic movement. The other factors are the rise during this whole period of the two independent disciplines of psychology and anthropology. And these factors can hardly be

[1] Cf. F. J. Hoffman, *Freudianism and the Literary Mind* (Baton Rouge, 1957), pp. 297–313, for a discussion of this issue.

considered in isolation. The radical changes in man's view of himself in the twentieth century brought about by these two latter disciplines was in large measure foreshadowed in imaginative literature and the arts generally but particularly in the literature and theory of the romantic movement with its sympathetic emphasis on the sub-rational, intuitive and instinctive aspects of personality. Romantic literature hence paved the way for these new insights and even after its initial enthusiasm had passed and reactions had set in the romantic movement had permanently modified and extended man's sense of himself in ways which would make the insights of psychology and anthropology more readily assimilable. It is logical then to consider firstly the impact of the romantic movement on primitivism.

In her study of primitivism in *Sturm und Drang* literature, Edith A. Runge isolates many qualities which *mutatis mutandis* are equally evident in English romanticism; qualities that may be largely summed up as the acceptance of a certain view of external 'nature' and a corresponding view of the 'natural' in man as a moral and emotional centre of value (cf. *Primitivism and Related Ideas in Sturm und Drang Literature*, pp. 1–46). But the parallel applies with particular importance in her general conclusion that the crucial factor distinguishing the primitivist tendencies of this period from the earlier conventions of the golden age, the pastoral, or the noble savage is a shift of emphasis from the external situation to the internal state (ibid., pp. ix–x). Whereas earlier primitivist reference had worked generally on the assumption of human nature being a more or less passive entity that could be corrupted or ennobled according to its social or natural environment, the more common deduction to be drawn from the primitivist tendencies of the romantics was that the essential difference was now an inner or psychological affair. The new relation to the natural world was essentially a state of mind.

This distinction may be made clearer if we consider the

conclusions of H. N. Fairchild in *The Noble Savage* and Lois Whitney in *Primitivism and the Idea of Progress*. Both of these studies follow the fortunes of eighteenth-century primitivist conventions into the early nineteenth century and note their remarkable falling off. In both cases, however, the author's interest is in the eighteenth-century convention rather than primitivism more broadly considered and taking a larger view it seems that this falling off can be seen not simply as the discarding of the fads and fashions of a previous age but more positively as their being supplanted by the more profound manifestations of primitivist feeling in the central figures of English romanticism. The key figure here is clearly Wordsworth whose contribution is helpfully summarized by M. H. Abrams in *The Mirror and the Lamp* (New York, 1953, p. 296).

> Wordsworth's special achievement is nearer to being unique, for in some of his most effective passages he not only vivifies the natural scene, but seems to revert to the very patterns of thought and feeling memorialized in communal myths and folk-lore. Coleridge explicitly maintained that Wordsworth, in the power of imagination, 'stands nearest of all modern writers to Shakespeare and Milton; and yet in a kind perfectly unborrowed and his own.' This characteristic and unborrowed power is found, not in Wordsworth's formal mythological poems, but in the many passages (of which several are cited by Coleridge) in which his imagination, rejecting all hereditary symbols, and without violence to the truth of perception, operates as myth in process rather than on myth in being.

Abrams's distinction between Wordsworth's 'formal mythological poems' and his recreation of mythic feeling and thought recognizes the, as it were, residual continuance of primitivist conventions of the more formal literary kind while at the same time indicating the more profound and inward mode of primitivist expression classically exemplified in Wordsworth.

The emphasis, then, has shifted from primitivism as a conventional location such as the rural retreat or the Pacific paradise to primitivism as a mode of sensibility. And one of the implications of this shift from outer to inner is that the new sense of the relation to external nature or to the instinctual self no longer requires a chronologically remote or pre-civilized world for its realization. Indeed, rather than implying an absolutely opposite alternative to civilization the primitive can be manifest as a suffusive quality of feeling within the civilized identity. The interest lies now in a merging rather than a polarization of qualities and whatever his external situation an individual may possess or develop from within himself the desiderated qualities of sensibility. There may, of course, be situations, such as that of the peasant, or stages in life, such as childhood, which are peculiarly favourable to such a state of mind, but the accent now falls on the different mode of feeling and response as a universal potentiality of human nature. This means that without needing to be overtly primitivist at the level of setting or conscious reference such literature recreates modes of feeling and a relation to the outside world for which the anthro- pological concepts of natural piety and animism are the nearest analogues.

It is apparent that the features discussed in *The Rainbow* and *Moby Dick* are related to this aspect of the romantic tradition. Indeed, Melville himself suggests the connection when he refers in *Moby Dick* to the albatross of Coleridge's *The Rime of the Ancient Mariner*, that other white sea-creature whose death is such an offence to the natural pieties, and Lydia Lensky's experience among the trees closely parallels Wordsworth's sensitivity to 'unknown modes of being' as described by Abrams. In fact, the difference between Coleridge's highly intellectual self-conscious- ness and Wordsworth's deeply intuitive sensibility is reminiscent of the different creative approaches of Melville and Lawrence as outlined earlier. Both Coleridge and Melville give the impression of a highly self-conscious philosophical pursuit of elusive qualities of experience that Wordsworth and Lawrence, their mutual differences notwithstanding, seem at some point in their lives to have spontaneously enjoyed in their own ways. However, our present interest lies in the underlying community of interest and endeavour that these differences of temperament and intellectual standpoint throw into relief. Without dwelling further on this well documented aspect of romanticism we may fittingly sum it up in Abrams's words: 'Symbolism, animism and mythopoeia, in richly diverse forms, explicit or submerged, were so pervasive in this age as to constitute the most pertinent single attribute for defining romantic poetry.' (*The Mirror and the Lamp*, p. 296.) A full account of literary background here would involve also a discussion of the American tradition with which Lawrence was so familiar and for which *Moby Dick* provides the culmination. Suffice it to say that a body of literature exhibiting broadly romantic modes of sensibility is the obviously indispensable background for such works as *Moby Dick* and *The Rainbow*.

Abrams's comment that such elements as he describes could be 'explicit or submerged' in romantic poetry is interesting in the light of our discussion of the later development of primitivism; and once again the development of Lawrence's *œuvre* is especially instructive. We have seen that there is a strong affinity between what we might call his romantic and his primitivist phases and that the shift from one to the other is largely a matter of making 'explicit' what was formerly 'submerged'. His career up to and including *The Rainbow* may be seen as a progressive rediscovery in his own terms of essential elements of the romantic tradition and much of his later primitivism represents his frequently desperate attempt to recapture something of that world view by an effort of will when the spontaneity of the former state was lost. It is precisely at the point in his career at which the romantic faith of *The Rainbow* gives way to the bitterness of *Women in Love* that Lawrence begins to make overtly primitivist use of his anthropological reading. Just as

Wordsworth's romantic sensibility undermined more self-consciously primitivist conventions, so self-conscious primitivist reference seèms to have asserted itself in Lawrence's case as the confidence of his romantic world view was weakened. Lawrence's career in other words gives one line of derivation for modern primitivism; it is the assertion in his case of a beleaguered romanticism. We may put this more generally. The romantic movement provided the precedent for the literary recreation of psychological states whose qualities, putatively at least, were commonly lacking in the civilized personality. Later primitivism is the heir to this tradition except that where the romantics generally sought a unification of sensibility primitivist works have tended to dramatize the disintegration. Even when attempting to assimilate or come to sympathetic terms with the instinctual self primitivist literature generally presents it under an alien, frequently horrifying, aspect. The two main categories of primitivism discussed in this study can be seen then as different poles of reaction to the romantic ideal. Whereas the recreation of primitive sensibility is a direct descendant from the romantic example, conscious primitivism represents sympathetically or otherwise, the failure of the romantic aspiration. As we move along the scale from the recreation of primitive sensibility to the conscious use of primitive motifs so we move from Lawrence's direct affinity with the romantic tradition through Conrad's horrified fascination for the instinctual towards the possibility of attitudes such as those of T. S. Eliot and William Golding which are distinctly anti-romantic.

The interest in primitive life in the works discussed represents, then, both the continuation of the romantic tradition and a quizzical view of it, and the developments I have suggested have been given a further impetus by the concurrent interest in anthropology and psychology. Both of these sciences, for example, increased the self-consciousness of the new primitivist expressions that had replaced earlier conventions. Abrams's anthropological gloss of Coleridge's remarks on Wordsworth's poetry indicates a theoretical awareness of the nature of primitive sensibility that was not available to Wordsworth in that way. And as I have suggested at some length, the factor of theoretical self-consciousness can radically modify the internal chemistry of primitivist literature. We may usefully consider, then, in what ways psychology and anthropology can be said to have 'influenced' such literature.

One important effect of the rise of anthropology was to give documentary support to the romantic sense that the essential difference between the civilized and more primitive or 'natural' states is as much a different mode of the inner life as a different external situation, for it has been a common anthropological opinion that the psychology of the primitive mind is radically different from that of civilized man. We must tread carefully here since argument on precisely this point has been a *cause célèbre* of anthropology. The early anthropologist Sir James Frazer, for example, was not concerned with the enormous psychological differences suggested by the school of thought summarized in Cassirer. Indeed, Frazer's whole endeavour was to elucidate the universal patterns of human thought behind apparent divergences. And the contemporary theorist, Lévi-Strauss, though in a very different way, also emphasizes the universality of mental laws. None the less, as was evident from the Cassirer passage, there has been a strong element in anthropological thought which saw a radical divergence between the two states and for anyone inclined to view the matter in that light such a belief would not lack of apparent substantiation. From such a standpoint even the account of primitive beliefs and practices in *The Golden Bough* would be likely to substantiate the sense of a thoroughly alien world view. The universal laws of the mind require some unearthing while the immediate imaginative suggestiveness of the documentation is headily exotic and remote from civilized preconceptions. To a reader inclined to view the matter in this way, then, the progressive documentation of ritual and magic, totem and taboo, even when this is not the intention of the writer, may suggest the very different inner world of the real savage as opposed to the Utopian simplicities implied in the use of the golden age and noble savage conventions. Fairchild remarks of Southey, who earlier in the century had done considerable reading on real primitives, that 'as might be expected, the more Southey knows about the real savage the less he believes in the Noble Savage.' (*The Noble Savage*, p. 209.) By the latter end of the century it would seem that anthropology had not only seen the passing of the noble savage but had provided him with a more challenging successor. The new savage represented not just an alternative life situation but a totally different mode of feeling and mental disposition. To judge by the works discussed above, this sense of the primitive as having a radically different mentality seems to have been the aspect that has caught the imagination of literary artists.

The influential view that the primitive psychology is radically different from the civilized not only supports the romantic belief in a comparable polarity in modes of mental life but it leads to a similarly ambivalent interpretation. From the more positive viewpoint it is theoretically possible for anyone to enjoy the more primitive mentality if he can make the necessary inner adjustment. But by the same token it is impossible for anyone with a too exclusively civilized or analytic mode of mental life. Since for Wordsworth or Coleridge this was a polarity of theoretically available cultural choices then the problem lay mainly in reconciling them. In anthropological contexts, however, the corresponding polarity has a more chronological or evolutionary implication suggesting the impossibility of reconciliation. Edward B. Tylor in his *Primitive Culture* speaks in evolutionary terms of the difficulty of enjoying mythic and analytic mentality simultaneously: 'There is a kind of intellectual frontier within which he must be who will sympathize with myth, while he must be without it who will investigate it, and it is our fortune that we live near this frontierline and can go in and out.' (vol. I, ch. 9, p. 317.) Tylor's remark that he and his contemporaries can 'go in and out' implies only that at that historical moment there were sufficient primitive peoples to be available for study by the civilized rather than that the two states could be simultaneously experienced by the same individual. This psychological polarity, then, reflects the romantic notion that we 'murder to dissect', that the analytic intellect is achieved at the expense of a more primitive spontaneity and wholeness, and lends it the further implication that the primitive is more alien and remote. In other words there were strains in anthropological thinking which appeared to substantiate the sense we derive from primitivist literature that the primitive is a psychological potentiality the realization of which would imply the destruction of the civilized psyche. The romantic wholeness seems less and less possible.

But this question of the use to which writers have put anthropological knowledge raises a radical issue that has been begged throughout the preceding discussion. While indicating the literary modes and motifs that have invited the description 'primitivist' I have spoken of anthropological accounts of primitive man as if these comprised a firm consensus of opinion. Even in the preceding discussion, however, it has become increasingly apparent that this is not in fact the case. Not only have anthropological knowledge and theory developed enormously over the last hundred years or so but at any particular moment there have been and still are widely divergent schools of thought. The present day anthropology of Lévi-Strauss,[1] for example, argues a view of the primitive's capacity to handle complex abstract distinctions in matters of kinship and taboo which gives a very different picture from the once widely held belief in the non-analytic quality of primitive thought, the view summarized by Cassirer. Given the terms of

[1] *The Savage Mind*, trans. Weidenfeld & Nicolson (London, 1966).

reference of each discussion these views may not be as irreconcilable as this suggests but the important point is that Lévi-Strauss's account does not lend itself to the same kind of imaginative use. And given the inferential nature of all our supposed knowledge of the primitive mind we may question its validity both in the writer who uses anthropological motifs and in the critic who sees 'anthropological' qualities in, for example, *The Rainbow* or *The Prelude*. The entire anthropological background of the preceding discussions, in other words, is highly questionable.

It is worth emphasizing, therefore, that the strictly scientific validity of such material is not of final importance critically. The influence of anthropology on criticism is a complicated issue to be taken up in the next chapter but it can be noted here that the reading of mythic sensibility into *The Rainbow* or *The Prelude* is of importance not so much for its possible anthropological validity as for the insight such a comparison provides into modern man's interest in his primitive self by whatever path he has tried to approach it. And as far as creative writers are concerned, I have already pointed out that a writer may make imaginative use of this material in a spirit opposed to that of its original anthropological context. Both anthropologists and creative writers have projected their versions of the primitive on to the strictly unknowable past and from our point of view what matters is not the scientific validity of either but the common area of intent and intuition that has made cross-fertilization possible. We are not obliged to accept the primitivist projections of modern writers literally any more than we do the science of Chaucer or Shakespeare. In short, the effect of anthropology on literature is not to make it more true in some non-literary sense but to provide the stimulus and the material for creating more complex imaginative worlds. As we have seen in relation to several works, the critical issue is not how accurately a writer may be said to use anthropological material but how well he gives it meaning within a coherent symbolic world.

Indeed, this rather murky relationship between anthropology and literature can be viewed in a more positive light; it was the very absence of a firm distinction in the comparatively undeveloped state of anthropology in the late nineteenth and early twentieth centuries that seems to have rendered it peculiarly suggestive and readily adaptable as literary material. A critic's reference to *The Golden Bough* as late as 1941 as being in the category of 'unclassifiable books' (Vickery, op. cit., p. 271) suggests how slowly the full appreciation of an independent science has developed and in the first decades of the century anthropology was so closely related to literary studies as to be a subsection of criticism. As Frazer's title suggests, his major work grew out of the investigation of the meaning of the golden bough in Virgil's *Aeneid*. Jane E. Harrison (*Ancient Art and Ritual*, London, 1911) used much of Frazer's documentation in tracing the origins of ancient Greek drama back to ritual roots and Gilbert Murray's interest in Greek thought similarly led him back to its primitive religious origins (*Four Stages of Greek Religion*, New York, 1912). In demonstrating the primitive strata of feeling embodied in so much extant literature such studies also suggested the possibility of a literary recreation of the primitive as in the dances and chants of *The Plumed Serpent* or the widespread interest in myth.

And apart from this general relation between literature and anthropology by which literature acquired a new psychological dimension, such early figures as Frazer and Tylor seem to have provided a more specific stimulus. It is clear that Frazer's attitude to his material is not one that would now pass as scientific neutrality. Quite apart from the moral or psychological implications that might be thought to derive from the tendency of his argument, his elegant literary manner moves easily and frequently into parenthetical moral observations. And this in itself is not so important as the assumptions it reveals concerning the primitive and the civilized states. He clearly works from the assumption that the primitive is *ipso facto* inferior. He speaks of the worldwide majority of basically primitive minds as 'a standing menace to civilization' and, despite his expressed respect for the primitive forbears to whose early mental endeavours we owe our own civilization, his final summing up of the primitive is of 'a melancholy record of human folly and error'. Similarly, Tylor in his concluding chapter suggests that the most important use of our knowledge of primitive life is to recognize and weed out its residual forms in our own time. The general effect of these works in short is to provide a wealth of illuminating information comprising a disturbing new perspective on human nature while at the same time affirming or assuming the superiority of contemporary civilization. To a writer profoundly at odds with this civilization, this would provide a rich and satisfying apple cart to overturn. The anthropologists themselves provided the evidence upon which their cultural preferences could be questioned or reversed just as their documentation of the vestigial survival of primitive thought and practice, particularly in European country life, provided a suggestive precedent for the recreation of the primitive in contemporary experience. Early anthropologists' lapses from strictly scientific cultural relativism provided not only a precedent but a challenge for a writer like Lawrence.

This applies to the theorists, Frazer and Tylor, whose interest was in general principles drawn from material amassed by earlier researchers in the field. There is, however, another broad category of anthropological investigation: that of collecting the first hand information without necessarily relating it to general theory. Such first hand involvement with primitive peoples provides a different but related precedent for primitivist writing. Lawrence, for example, before writing *The Plumed Serpent* knew Leo Frobenius's *The Voice of Africa* (London, 1913) and had recently read the American novelist Charles Lummis's *The Land of Poco Tiempo* (New York, 1893). In these two accounts of the peoples of West

Africa and South-west America respectively the writers not only give factual information but become involved in the difficulties of defining their own attitudes towards them. In this respect they are in the tradition of the travellers' reports of preceding centuries. Part of the fascination of these two works lies in the authors' assimilation of the cultural shock occasioned by the very different values and assumptions of these peoples whom the authors wish to present in a sympathetic light while at the same time finding in them much that is horrifying or exasperating. This personal involvement, which from a strictly anthropological view point, as in Frobenius's case, is really irrelevant to the argument, becomes for the primitivist writer a primary point of interest. The new importance being accorded to primitive man lends a corresponding intensity and significance to the European's traditionally mixed response to him and a writer like Lawrence in effect internalizes this conflict in anthropological values. The first systematic attempt of western man to come to terms with cultural worlds outside of the accepted 'great' centres of civilization gives a new edge to the creative writer's traditional questioning of his own cultural world.

In these various ways, then, anthropology lends a new impetus and complexity to primitivist writing. In general we may say that, unlike the noble savage of tradition, the new savage resists the comfortably conventional view of him by opposing it with a coherent and substantial world view of his own. And the important point here is not so much the new wealth of information, but that anthropology suggests the increasingly relativistic attitude that may be adopted towards the primitive. The effect of such scientific material is not that the primitivist work of literature becomes an anthropological, scientific thesis but that it acquires a new and subversive freedom of perspective. The range of attitudes and imaginative modes exemplified by the writers considered in this study may be associated with the fact that they almost all make use of anthropological knowledge without the intermediary of a recognized primitivist convention. The common factor in so many of these works is their anguished exploration of a dilemma rather than the conventionalized exposition of an established position and this consciously heuristic emphasis in the use of the primitivist motif is an attitude that parallels the rise of anthropology.

The problems of discussing the possible influence of a conflicting body of anthropological opinions on a disparate body of literature are even worse when we come to consider psychology, a discipline whose effects are felt so pervasively in twentieth-century thought. But the same general discriminations may be made concerning its literary use. As with anthropology, writers have tended to make use of it in their own way; possibly in a spirit entirely contrary to its original context. F. J. Hoffman in *Freudianism and the Literary Mind* has pointed out how frequently Freud has been taken up in a spirit quite different from his own intention (pp. 312–13). Freud, always essentially a doctor, wanted to bring all psychological life as far as possible to a conscious and rational, hence curable, level and had a fundamental hostility to the instinctual life of the id. It is not surprising, therefore, that in his study of primitive man, *Totem and Taboo*, he should have seen the beliefs and customs associated with primitive kinship as neurotic symptoms. Yet as Hoffman points out the assimilation of Freud's insights by poets and novelists has frequently been more sympathetic to the id. More important to many readers than his own careful qualifications was the sheer awareness of potential human nature opened up by Freud and his successors. Primitive beliefs and practices rather than being regarded as neurotic manifestations take on the positive importance of giving access to the most ancient and hidden parts of the personality. Psychology in general then endorses that internalization of the primitive state that we have seen to be characteristic of modern or post-romantic primitivism. However they each evaluate it, for writers such as Conrad and Lawrence the primitive clearly reveals the most profound self.

But the psychologist whose theories and attitudes are most sympathetic to such an interest in the primitive is, of course, C. G. Jung. As he himself puts it in 'Archaic Man': '. . . every civilized human being, however high his conscious development, is still an archaic man at the deeper levels of his psyche.' (*Collected Jung*, vol. 10, p. 51.) And Jung's attitude to the archaic and unconscious self is far more positive and trusting. Like Lawrence, Jung saw the First World War as the catastrophic result of contemporary civilized man's denial and distrust of the unconscious and instinctual self. Although much of Jung's own development of the Freudian insights was published rather later than most of the works discussed in this survey, he does suggest the kind of relation to the new psychological discoveries that informs such primitivism as we have been discussing. Indeed Jung, whose work includes so much general cultural critique, offers a retrospective comment on the period I have been discussing and suggests the extent to which scientific psychology is not so much the cause as rather itself only one of many manifestations of a contemporary preoccupation with unconscious life among which we might number the preoccupation with the primitive.

> Yet he [modern man] is somehow fascinated by the almost pathological manifestations from the hinterland of the psyche, difficult though it is for us to explain how something which all previous ages have rejected should suddenly become interesting. That there is a general interest in these matters cannot be denied, however much it offends against good taste. I am not thinking merely of the interest taken in psychology as a science, or of the still narrower interest in the psychoanalysis of Freud, but of the widespread and ever-growing interest in all sorts of psychic phenomena, including spiritualism, astrology, Theosophy, parapsychology, and so forth. The world has seen nothing like it since the end of the seventeenth century. We can compare it only to the flowering of Gnostic thought in the first and

second centuries after Christ. The spiritual currents of our time have, in fact, a deep affinity with Gnosticism. There is even an 'Église gnostique de la France', and I know of two schools in Germany which openly declare themselves Gnostic. The most impressive movement numerically is undoubtedly Theosophy, together with its continental sister, Anthroposophy; these are pure Gnosticism in Hindu dress. Compared with them the interest in scientific psychology is negligible.

(*Collected Jung*, vol. 10, p. 83)

The popularity of these movements was high at the turn of the present century and all my examples of primitivism bear a close relation to Jung's general category of fascination with 'the almost pathological manifestations from the hinterland of the psyche'. And Theosophy, as made available in Mme Blavatsky's *The Secret Doctrine* and *Isis Unveiled*, was enormously influential on the works of such major figures as Joyce, Yeats and Lawrence.

The modern primitivism discussed in this study, then, is part of a general concern in the late nineteenth and early twentieth centuries with the subconscious mind and anti-rational modes of understanding. It exhibits assumptions and motifs that can be related particularly to the concurrent development of anthropology and psychology. Yet the problems of suggesting anything but the most generalized influences in these connections may be illustrated from the different attitudes of T. S. Eliot and Lawrence to Frazer. Where Eliot speaks respectfully in his notes to *The Wasteland* of his indebtedness to a work that has 'profoundly influenced' his generation, Lawrence eyes askance Frazer's method of theorizing from his study rather than from direct experience and when he does approve Frazer's argument it is only for its confirmation of his own independent insights:

I have been reading Frazer's *Golden Bough* and *Totemism and Exogamy*. Now I am convinced of what I believed when I was about twenty – that there is another seat of consciousness than the brain and the nerve system: there is a blood-consciousness which exists in us independently of the ordinary mental consciousness, which depends on the eye as its source or connector.[1]

Lawrence's explication here makes it apparent that as so often he is not so much agreeing as placing his own interpretation or emphasis on his reading. Where Eliot's use of *The Golden Bough* depends on its publicly recognized meaning and significance, Lawrence assimilates it parenthetically into the highly personal intuitions already embodied in his work. Hence the importance of discriminating between the different imaginative worlds into which these general 'influences' are assimilated. As this comparison suggests, writers such as Lawrence and Melville whose interest in the primitive is so much derived from their own sensibility and first hand experience will be more difficult to deal with in terms of 'influence' than one who can actually advertise the sources of his poetic material and questions of precise indebtedness can only be pursued usefully, therefore, in relation to individual authors. The present chapter suggests then some major factors which have affected modern primitivism while the preceding discussions of individual works should indicate something of the different uses to which it has been put.

[1] *The Collected Letters of D. H. Lawrence*, 2 vols, ed. Harry T. Moore (London, 1962), p. 393.

4
The Primitivism of the Critics

The preceding chapters have suggested some guidelines for discussing a literary tendency that ranges from works of such explicitly primitive reference and concern as *Heart of Darkness* to the 'submerged' recreation of mythic feeling that characterizes much romantic literature. Besides overt primitivism, in other words, there is a broad imaginative category in which the characteristic modes of feeling and perception have invited a primitivist, or at least anthropological, frame of reference. It seems, therefore, worth rounding off my comments on the intellectual context of modern primitivism by pointing out some current critical tendencies which have applied this primitivist or anthropological perspective to literature on a more general scale. There is in fact a long-standing tradition by which primitive man has been seen as intrinsically poetical but this conventional idea has received a new twist from twentieth-century anthropological perspectives. Apart from anthropological investigations of specific origins of the kind exemplified by Jane Harrison and briefly mentioned in the preceding chapter, there is a frequent tendency in modern critical theory to regard all literature as essentially a form of myth; as the recreation in effect of a primitive world view. Literature, seen in this light, is valued for its capacity to make available an ancient mode of thought that cuts across, perhaps, our habitual mental predispositions. Once again this may be seen under two different though not mutually exclusive aspects. There are theories in which literature is seen as the use of mythic forms and others in which it is seen as the recreation of mythic sensibility. We may consider first the latter and less influential of these.

Various anthropological theories as well as Ernst Cassirer's illuminating studies of the cognitive function of non-discursive symbolic forms have provided a stimulus and a theoretical groundwork for speculations such as Wayne Shumaker's in *Literature and the Irrational*. Arguing from what have long been recognized as the generally subrational modes of literary language and forms Shumaker suggests that literature puts the reader into a special state of mind similar to that which characterizes primitive modes of thought as outlined by Cassirer and other authorities. Having recounted, for example, an Australian mythical explanation of pregnancy he goes on to comment:

> How consistent such a pattern of meaning percepts is with patterns common in literature can be seen if we convert the belief into story. For example: one day it happened that a chief's daughter, who passed near the stone while deeply preoccupied, became pregnant. Now the spirit which just then was waiting at the orifice chanced to be that of the chief's bitterest enemy, who had recently been killed in furious battle with eight of his followers; so the child when born. . . . Already the spell of fictive adventure begins to fall upon us. The 'impossible' assumptions cease to trouble us as they enter into combination with other elements that can be projected from them. In its living context, the superstition was credible because it formed part of a huge nexus of supporting beliefs. In the literary version, a nexus, all the parts of which are conditioned by it, can be created around the superstition in such a way as to suspend the entire complex in a 'virtual' world which we can enter imaginatively by choice. The *quality* of the primitive nexus and of the literary nexus is similar, for in both what feels right is convincing and acceptable, regardless of whether it is immediately justifiable to reason.[1]

The argument here, which is clearly different from 'anthropological' discussions of certain romantic texts or of Greek tragedy,

---

[1] Wayne Shumaker, *Literature and the Irrational: A Study in Anthropological Backgrounds*, p. 37. © 1960. Reprinted by permission of Prentice-Hall Inc., Englewood Cliffs, N.J.

seems forced to me since it implies that associational or intuitional modes of thought are somehow specifically primitive while not taking sufficient account of the highly self-conscious mental poise that accompanies the reading of literature. A 'willing suspension of disbelief' must be of a very different order from naive belief and the very fact of 'a "virtual" world into which we can enter imaginatively by choice' must affect our involvement in the 'literary nexus'. I hope it is not unfair to quote this passage in isolation from the argument, which is, of course, qualified and substantiated in other ways, for the objection remains, it seems to me, that a potentially interesting parallel is drawn without there being any way of coping with the intellectual problems that it raises. For present purposes, however, this passage in its very explicitness is usefully symptomatic. The suggestion that literature recreates the archaic state of mind is reminiscent of Robert Graves's assertion that all lyric poetry derives from an ancient stratum of feeling, or as he puts it, is addressed to the White Goddess (*The White Goddess*, New York, 1948). Literature gains in profundity, is the implication, if it can be related to primitive emotional experience. The most convincing and influential example of this critical tendency is Maud Bodkin's *Archetypal Patterns in Poetry*, but this is because, for all its more generalized suggestiveness, it limits itself to specific and well illustrated examples of the recreation of mythic feeling and archetypal forms. Apart from Bodkin such theory has had little influence and I mention it as one aspect of a primitivist tendency in modern critical thinking; the honorific value accorded to the mythic or primitive *per se*.

The more influential manifestation of this, also in some measure derived from Bodkin, is that which sees literature not so much as the recreation of mythic mentality in this inward sense but rather as a mythic cartography of human experience. Bodkin's brilliant analysis of archetypal patterns in poetry has been taken up in a more systematic way by the Canadian critic, Northrop Frye, who

sees the whole of literature as the perpetual recreation of fundamental myths and archetypes.[1] 'Systematic' is the key term here
for Frye's theory implies more than the random use of specific
myths, such as the Prometheus story, or archetypes, such as the
mother archetype. He sees the whole of literature as contained
within four basic 'modes' of comedy, romance, tragedy and satire,
which collectively comprise a mythic representation of human
experience on the overall model of the fall and the expulsion from
Eden. The shift of emphasis here from the specific recreation of
mythic archetypes and patterns to a generalized theory is crucial
for it means that, whatever the individual qualities of feeling in a
work may be, its status as a literary mode is enough to imbue it
with this radical mythic dimension. Frye, it is true, explicitly dis-
claims an anthropological validity for his system and presents it as
a purely logical and inductive framework. But as his objecters
point out, the system derives much of its charisma from the lurking implication that these logical categories are more profound
psychologically than the traditional generic distinctions. There is a
covert assumption that the cartography of the imagination embodied in the literary modes has a life of myth as well as a simply
classificatory utility. It should be said that in Frye's hands, when
informed in other words with his own wide reading and critical
perceptiveness, this way of looking at literature has been illuminating. My reservations lie at a more theoretical level, for Frye, while
himself deprecating the excesses of myth criticism, in effect provides theoretical support for a critical disposition which in its
broader manifestations, particularly in much North American practice, has its unfortunate side. There is a widespread assumption that
the detection of mythic elements or the application of the modal
perspective automatically confers interest or value on a work. The

[1] Cf. especially *Anatomy of Criticism* (Princeton University Press, 1957) for a
comprehensive account of Frye's critical theory and *The Educated Imagination*
(Indiana University Press, 1964) for a briefer and more popular account, which also
gives a sense of its practical application to the teaching of literature.

term 'myth' is the blank cheque of honorific commentary. In so far as this promotes a medium of discussion in which traditional considerations of humane and intellectual judgement are overriden by the mere invocation of the term 'myth' this seems to me an extremely reductive kind of primitivist assumption. And 'assumption' seems the relevant word here, for the overt fascination with the primitive exemplified in Lawrence or Conrad is the top of an iceberg of less definite or obvious tendencies of feeling and intellectual disposition to which, it seems, many persons of a literary inclination are perhaps peculiarly prone. Is it possible that the critical consideration of the primitivist impulse in its more overt forms in literature may help to create a more critical awareness of such surreptitious or 'armchair' primitivism in readers?

5
Conclusion and Further Directions

In this discussion I have applied a consistent principle of discrimination to compare and, I hope, throw some critical light on widely different uses of an amorphous body of motif and reference. Whether it be animism, natural piety, myth, ritual or reference to ancient or pre-civilized cultures, the primitivist material has no absolute meaning; it acquires its significance in terms of the artist's own vision. The foregoing comparisons should make plain just how varied the moral, philosophic and artistic assumptions of these visions may be. There is not even the loose affinity that we might find in the romantics or the symbolist poets. Hence, the aim of this survey is not comprehensiveness but variety. It suggests a range of possibilities and one way of coping with them. I hope, however, that this study will suggest useful critical pointers to other writers who, though not mentioned here, might well be discussed in this general connection. A critical starting point, for example, for dealing with the primitivist elements in Virginia Woolf's *Between the Acts*, say, or Saul Bellow's *Henderson the Rain King* would be to note, in the spirit of the present study, the high degree of self-consciousness on the part of the author in Woolf's case or of the character himself in the Bellow. Such considerations of primitivist motifs, which do seem to me potentially illuminating, are only possible on the basis of some such terms of reference.

Similarly, my discussion of Lawrence's very conscious use of Mexico and Conrad's of Africa suggests a strategy that occurs more widely in modern literature. E. M. Forster and Joyce Cary, for example, have frequently made use of a foreign culture or national character as the embodiment of a mental and psychological disposition which they have clearly felt to be radically different from that of their own countrymen. One naturally hesitates to use the term 'primitivist' in a context that might be thought to imply an unfortunate reflection on the still almost contemporary societies of India, Italy and Africa used by these authors; and in the case of *A Passage to India* such an implication would be especially inappropriate. But the fictional use of the national culture and psychology does stem from a very similar impulse to the primitivist. Cary's Africa and Forster's Italy clearly represent something of the spontaneity for which, mistakenly or not, primitive man has so often been prized. Such uses of foreign cultures have a ready affinity with primitivism as we have been discussing it.

Lawrence's interest in America also raises the large and complex consideration that the new world, in both the European and the American imagination, has itself always had strongly primitivist associations. For all his ineradicable Englishness and his detestation of the modern United States, Lawrence was an adoptive American in his fascination with the ancient races and the great literature of America. His *Studies in Classic American Literature* is not only the first major recognition of a cohesive cultural identity in American literature; it is also in itself a primitivist quest. Lawrence's adoption, as it were, of the American tradition is as revealing in this respect as T. S. Eliot's adoption of a European identity. And in Lawrence's later primitivism, there emerge two of the major primitivist features of the American literary tradition: the sense of a natural world somehow more vast and untamed than that of Europe and the theme of the interrelations between the white man and the older races of the continent. These features, classically expressed in Fenimore Cooper and Melville, are equally discernible in the more recent writer William Faulkner. The initiation of Ike McCaslin in *The Bear*, for example, and the use of the negro to express a psychological opposite to the white man are squarely in this tradition. Whereas the primitivist examples

G

considered in this study have cropped up for the most part very randomly, the American tradition comes close to providing a cohesive body of primitivist literature. Yet, here too, critical discriminations comparable to those I have been making would be necessary in considering a tradition encompassing such different spirits as the eighteenth-century Crèvecoeur and a modern such as Faulkner.

All these suggestions, however, are only general pointers to some important directions that primitivist feeling has taken and it is clearly more appropriate at this juncture to indicate some of the limits of the topic. The general implication of this study has been that primitivism denotes, or arises from, a sense of crisis in civilization. Indeed, unless we choose to include the literary productions of actual primitives, such as form the material of C. M. Bowra's *Primitive Song* (New York, 1962), primitivism is always by definition the paradoxical product of civilization itself. Primitivism, then, is born of the interplay between the civilized self and the desire to reject or transform it. This interplay, as we have seen, may take a positive or creative direction. In Lawrence, for example, there is a recreation within the civilized consciousness of very primary levels of feeling; a mingling of both to produce that spontaneity and emotional fullness so superbly embodied in his best works. Or, as in Golding, this interplay may be a clash; like the clash between the technological sophistication of the motor car or modern weapons and the primitively aggressive emotions these machines can be used to express. But either way the characteristic domain of primitivism is the interplay between two modes of being assumed to be either incompatible or in some sense mutually repellent. Primitivism, we might say, is the projection by the civilized sensibility of an inverted image of the self. Its characteristic focus is the gap or tension that subsists between these two selves and its most characteristic resultant is impasse.

This sense of impasse, the recognition of the contradictory

nature of the primitivist impulse, provides I think the most useful point of reference for the modern works we have been discussing as primitivist. In so far as a work suggests a resolution of the primitivist paradox, a genuine rapprochement between the primitive and the civilized, so it begins to invite a different term such as 'romantic'. Lawrence, I have suggested, is the best exemplification of this with his shift from romantic to primitivist paralleled by the shift from faith to desperation. And in order to clarify more fully this borderline area of the whole topic, it may help to consider briefly Henry Miller; a professed heir to Lawrence. In *The Mind and Art of Henry Miller* (Baton Rouge, 1967), W. A. Gordon speaks frequently of Miller's 'primitivism' and more generally of his relation to the romantic tradition. Gordon is referring here to Miller's radical shedding of moral and social preconceptions to make, as it were, a naked encounter with the whole life of the psyche, even that which the civilized consciousness is commonly supposed to suppress or ignore. This rediscovery of identity by a willed, and indeed joyous, abandonment to the instinctual self, is the romantic aspect of Miller and primitivism is the means or occasion for this. One can see Gordon's point here and would not, I think, wish to quarrel with his use of the term primitive in his specific contexts. I think it would be misleading, though, to use this term more generally of Miller, for although Miller's moral and psychological endeavour may be related to the concerns and attitudes which have produced primitivist literature, there are good reasons why he does not characteristically attempt to recreate the feel of a pre-civilized sensibility or rely heavily on overtly primitivist motifs. The whole force of what Miller does resides in his use of a modern American male as his narrating persona and his use of modern urban life. These are both, of course, used in a heightened, at times surrealistic, way but even within this visionary mode contemporary urban life is always recognizable. Miller does not in fact set up a primitive alternative to the civilized because, I think, he would not accept the polarity that this implies. Where Conrad, for example, opposes the primitive and the civilized, the restrained and the unrestrained, for Miller this conflict of values or personal identities does not occur. His protagonist has in his own sphere the freedom of Kurtz or Don Ramón in theirs, yet without the qualifying presence of Marlowe or Kate Leslie. Miller does not resolve the dilemmas of Conrad and Lawrence, he simply denies them by placing his whole work in a frame of visionary subjectivism. By the same token, he does not require an alienating symbol for his instinctual self because he accepts this self so totally. Miller is not a primitivist, in short, because he does not need to be.

In their different ways, then, both Miller and Lawrence suggest the border area of primitivism. Within the general framework of romanticism, they have both indicated a positive rapprochement of the primitivist, or at least anti-civilized, impulse and the sophisticated identity. We might say that such a broadly romantic resolution, the internal assimilation of the primitive, lies on one side of the primitivist dilemma and the purely conventional, metaphorical use of the primitive, as in Eliot or the Noble Savage, lies on the other. And as we move in this way outside the narrower area of primitivist literature we come back to our starting point. Having opened this study with a comment on the universality of primitivist nostalgia and the corresponding difficulty of assigning clear limits to it even as a purely literary phenomenon, it is as well to close with the same reminder. A full discussion of primitivism as a cultural phenomenon could properly lead to such topics as the twentieth-century popularity of sun-bathing or the contemporary phenomenon of the hippie commune and, as is particularly evident in the case of Lawrence, there is considerable interplay between such sociological tendencies and the insights of imaginative literature.

Of course, I have neither the space nor the competence to explore further such sociological manifestations of the primitivist impulse. There is, however, one general question that rises naturally from this whole discussion and which may suggest in closing how the problems of primitivism change and yet endure. Walter J. Ong in *The Barbarian Within* (p. 282) suggests that the complex of attitudes expressed in the etymology of the word 'barbarian', attitudes by which the notions of 'foreign' and 'uncivilized' become largely interchangeable, is finally giving way to a 'global consciousness'. Though we may still encounter the savage in our own personalities, we are less and less able to project him on to some other national or racial group. This must affect the possibility of writing primitivist literature of the kind that comprises much of the material of this study, even though such literature makes generally honorific use of foreign peoples. Not only does a white writer, one imagines, feel some diffidence in the present social climate about making any kind of overtly primitivist use of, say, one of the darker races but the situation is in any case largely taken out of his hands by, for example, American blacks expressing with considerable vigour and articulacy their own sense of what it is to be a negro. It seems that on the one hand an external projection of the primitive on to others is less possible while on the other hand the questioning of the civilized self is, if anything, more radical and inward than ever. Not only the moral subversiveness of Henry Miller and similar imaginative writers but the psychological critiques of civilization in Norman O. Brown (*Life Against Death*, London, 1959) and Herbert Marcuse (*Eros and Civilization*, Boston, 1955) testify to this latter fact. If the history of primitivism from ancient times, through romanticism, to the early twentieth century is one of a progressively more inward and anguished location of the civilized dilemma then this tendency seems to be continuing unabated in our own time.

Select Bibliography

There is no standard work that attempts to treat this topic comprehensively. Since I have concentrated on modern texts the following selection includes as well as some general discussions several historical surveys covering periods up to the romantic. Most of these historical studies are in the Lovejoy tradition of documentation rather than critical analysis.

BAIRD, JAMES, *Ishmael: A Study of the Symbolic Mode in Primitivisim*, Baltimore, 1956.
Illuminating account of late nineteenth-century novelists' interest in Oceania as a response to the waning authority of Christian symbolism.

BOAS, GEORGE, *Essays on Primitivism and Related Ideas in the Middle Ages*, Baltimore, 1948.
Surveys primitivist expression in medieval Christian thought. Despite modifications a tradition survives from antiquity to the Renaissance.

BODKIN, MAUD, *Archetypal Patterns in Poetry*, London, 1934.
Illuminating application of psychological and anthropological insights to literature. Mythic forms and feeling always demonstrated within the works.

CASSIRER, ERNST, *The Philosophy of Symbolic Forms* (3 vols), trans. Ralph Manheim, New Haven, Conn., 1953, 1955, 1957.
Most comprehensive account of Cassirer's view of man's development as a symbol-making creature and of the relation between the primitive and the developed minds. The second volume is especially concerned with mythic mentality.

CHINARD, G., *L'Amérique et le Rêve Exotique*, Paris, 1913.

Suggests the primitivist significance of America in French thought from its discovery and traces the absorption of this primitivist tradition in Rousseau.

FAIRCHILD, H. N., *The Noble Savage*, New York, 1928.

Readable survey of the use of this idea from the eighteenth into the nineteenth century. Notes the decline of the convention in the early nineteenth century.

FITZGERALD, M. M., *First Follow Nature*, New York, 1947.

Concentrates on lesser poets between 1725 to 1750. While its limited scope is regrettable this historical cross-section shows the varied and popular nature of primitivist expression at the time.

FRAZER, JAMES G., *The Golden Bough* (revised), 3rd ed., London, 1911–15 (first pub. London and New York, 1890).

Though this anthropological classic, which 'profoundly influenced' Eliot's generation, is now completely dated, it should be read not only as the great source book of modern literature but for its incidental revelation of cultural assumptions.

GOLDWATER, ROBERT, *Primitivism in Modern Art* (revised), New York, 1967.

Useful companion study of primitivist expression in a different medium. A comparison reveals mainly the differences; the facility of literature, for example, in exploring and defining the moral complexities of primitivist positions.

HOFFMAN, F. J., *Freudianism and the Literary Mind* (2nd ed.), Baton Rouge, 1957.

This study of the impact of Freud on modern writers includes some general discussion of primitivist and anti-rational trends in the period.

KERMODE, FRANK, ed., *The Tempest*, London, 1964.

The introduction brings together a discussion of the 'primitivist' sources and of the poetic mode of the play hence suggesting the imaginative *use* of this material.

86 PRIMITIVISM

The first eight essays in this collection touch usefully on the questions of myth, primitive thought, literature and criticism which have been discussed in the present study.

LEVIN, HARRY, *The Myth of the Golden Age in the Renaissance*, Indiana, 1969.

A helpful survey of primitivist or related expression in the renaissance.

LOVEJOY, A. O., and BOAS, G., *A Documentary History of Primitivism and Related Ideas in Antiquity*, Baltimore, 1934.

A compendious survey of primitivist expression in ancient Greece and Rome relying mainly on lengthy quotations.

MURRAY, H. A., ed., *Myth and Mythmaking*, New York, 1959.

ONG, WALTER J., *The Barbarian Within*, New York, 1962.

The title essay of this collection considers some of the broader cultural issues raised by the present study.

ROUSSEAU, J.-J., 'Discours sur l'Origine et les Fondements de l'Inégalité parmi les Hommes', *Oeuvres Complètes*, 23 vols, Paris, 1823 – 6, I, 223–318.

Since Rousseau is the figure most widely associated with primitivist ideas in Western thought, it is as well to be familiar with his actual position which is less simply primitivist than is often supposed.

RUNGE, EDITH A., *Primitivism and Related Ideas in Sturm und Drang Literature*, Baltimore, 1946.

A documentary survey in the Lovejoy tradition with some good insight into the effects of a romantic world view on primitivist expression.

RUTHVEN, K. K., 'The Savage God: Conrad and Lawrence', *Critical Quarterly*, X (1968), 39–54.

Places the primitivism of Lawrence and Conrad in its period though with rather different conclusions from mine.

TINDALL, WILLIAM YORK, *D. H. Lawrence and Susan his Cow*, New York, 1939.

Though of little critical value, this study provides useful documentation of Lawrence's interest in and reading about primitive life.

TYLOR, EDWARD B., *Primitive Culture*, London, 1871.

With Frazer this work provides a compendious account of late nineteenth-century understanding of and attitudes towards primitive man.

WHITNEY, LOIS, *Primitivism and the Idea of Progress*, Baltimore, 1934.

Suggests that the decline of eighteenth-century primitivist conventions is owing to the apparent vindication of the idea of progress in the nineteenth.

VICKERY, JOHN B., '*The Golden Bough* and Modern Poetry', *Journal of Aesthetics and Art Criticism*, XV, 3 (1957), 271–88.

A discussion of Yeats, Lawrence and Edith Sitwell with some general discussion of the relevance of Frazer to the contemporary situation.

Index

Lawrence, D. H.—*Cont.*
of primitivism, 38; identification with characters, 22; language and consciousness, 14–15; literalism, primitive, 39–41; ritual, use of, 17–19, 30, 36, 45; romanticism, 60, 61, 81; sensibility, 19–20, 41, 45, 46, 72; time, sense of, 15–16, 37
Leavis, F. R., 19, 40–1
Lévi-Strauss, C., 62, 64–5
Lord of the Flies (Golding) 53–4
Lovejoy, A. O., 47
Lummis, Charles, 67–8

Mann, Thomas, 43
Marcuse, Herbert, 83
Mardi (Melville), 21
Melville, Herman, 12, 20, 48–9, 59–60; animism of, 23–7; dramatization strategy, 21–5; experience and primitivism, 20–1, 72; mythic piety, 28; rationalism and fable, 22–5; ritual, use of, 28; romanticism and, 60; symbolic material, 21
Miller, Henry, 81–2, 83
Moby Dick (Melville), 20, 23–8, 30–1, 32, 60
Murder in the Cathedral (Eliot), 45

Murray, Gilbert, 66
myth (*see also* anthropology): affirmative use of, 45–8; archetypal patterns, 75–6; ironic use of by Eliot, 43–4, 46; continuity, cultural and, 42–3, 45, 48; literature and critical view of, 73–7; romanticism and, 60
mythic forms, critical theory of, 75–7
mythic sensibility, critical theory of, 73–5
Omoo (Melville), 20, 21
Ong, Walter J., 83

Passage to India, A (Forster), 79
piety, mythic, 10–11, 28–30, 35–6, 51–2
Pincher Martin (Golding), 54
Plumed Serpent, The (Lawrence), 32–42, 67
Prelude, The (Wordsworth), 65
Primitive Song (Bowra), 80
primitivism (*see also* conscious privitivism; sensibility, primitive or mythic): American, 79–83; anthropology and, 52, 56, 60, 61–9, 71–2; antirationalism and, 56; commitment to *v.* sympathy for, 39–41; crisis, cultural, and, 80–3;